JAMES I

ENGLISH MONARCHS TREASURES FROM THE NATIONAL ARCHIVES

JAMES I

The masque of monarchy

JAMES TRAVERS

THE NATIONAL ARCHIVES

First published in 2003 by

The National Archives
Kew, Richmond
Surrey TW9 4DU
UK

www.nationalarchives.gov.uk/

The National Archives was formed when the Public Record Office and
Historical Manuscripts Commission combined in April 2003

A catalogue record for this book is available from the British Library

ISBN 1 903365 56 2

Designed by Penny Jones and Michael Morris, Brentford, Middlesex

Printed in the UK by Butler and Tanner Ltd, Frome, Somerset

ILLUSTRATIONS

Cover: Detail from a portrait of James I, by Daniel Mytens, 1621;
Court of King's Bench: *Coram Rege* Roll (Easter Term, 1623);
(background) the second page of a letter from James authorizing the torture
of Guy Fawkes (see document 11).

Half-title page and page x (facing Preface): Portrait of James VI and I, by John Decritz.
This image matches written descriptions of James when he first came to his English
court. James habitually dressed more soberly than many of his courtiers, with only
details like the jewels in his hat proclaiming his status. This comparative plainness
served only to emphasize his importance, a grave figure presiding at the centre of
a brilliant throng of devotees.

Frontispiece: Detail from letters patent creating Henry Prince of Wales and Earl
of Chester, dated 4 June 1610 (see pp. 72–73).

Title page: James I's first Great Seal. This impression of the obverse shows the King
enthroned, between the arms of Cadwallader, last king of the Britons, and those of
Edward the Confessor. The arms emphasize James in his role as the uniter of ancient
kingdoms, British and Saxon.

Contents page: Illuminated initial from the Court of King's Bench: *Coram Rege* Roll
(Easter Term, 1623), see p. 56.

Contents

Acknowledgements

I would like to thank the following for their practical help and constructive suggestions:

Adrian Ailes, Amanda Bevan, Jane Crompton, Sean Cunningham, Catherine Guggiari, Malcolm Mercer, Deborah Pownall, Kathryn Sleight and Sarah Travers.

This book is dedicated to Sarah, and to my parents Martin and Veronica.

Series Note

Most of the key historic documents selected for this series are from the collections at The National Archives; a few are reproduced courtesy of other important national or private repositories.

Each key document is reproduced on a numbered double-page spread with an explanatory introduction placing it in context. (Selected pages or details have been chosen for lengthy items.) Transcripts, with modernized spellings and explanations of archaic words, are provided where necessary. All the documents featured on these spreads are cross-referenced in the main text.

If you would like to see the original documents at The National Archives at Kew, please see www.nationalarchives.gov.uk or phone 020 8392 5200 for information about how to obtain a free Reader's Ticket.

For further information about titles in the ENGLISH MONARCHS series or other publications from The National Archives, please send your name and address to:

Publications Marketing, FREEPOST SEA 7565, Richmond, Surrey, UK TW9 4DU (stamp required from overseas)

To order any publication from The National Archives, visit www.pro.gov.uk/bookshop/

The Documents

Preface

Although James VI of Scotland and I of England appears in this series on 'English' monarchs, his dual title reminds us that he was a Scottish king and then a British one. This study concentrates on James' reign in England, but looks at it in the light of his earlier reign in Scotland. James has been accused of an ignorance of the institutions of English government, but it can be argued that he brought to them the critical eye of a successful monarch from another country, who knew there were other ways of doing things. Many events and issues of James' reign are well known, but often only out of their historical context; these include the Union of the Crowns, the King James Bible, the Gunpowder Plot, his views on witchcraft and tobacco, the colonization of Virginia, the plantation of Ulster, the execution of Sir Walter Raleigh, and the flowering of drama at court and in the public theatres.

The 'masque' of the subtitle of this book perhaps needs a word of explanation. In one sense James' historical reputation is like a mask obscuring his true identity. He attracted flattery and malicious gossip in equal measure and this mixture has made his reign difficult to evaluate fairly. Until recently, historians have tended to dismiss the flattery and believe the gossip. This has fuelled a sometimes disparaging popular view of James today that focuses more on his supposed personal habits than on his competence as a king.

James adopted as many masks as his predecessor. Where Elizabeth had been Gloriana, Belphoebe or the Virgin Queen, James was the British Solomon, The Father of his People or Albion. In these guises he would sit as the focus of the masque proper, a courtly entertainment flourishing in James' reign, in which courtiers, disguised as abstract concepts such as Hope and Faith, portrayed ideals of kingship and conduct. Sometimes the symbolism went wrong: in one masque Hope and Faith got so drunk they were sick. Even when the players were sober the masque could be critical, showing the difference between the ideal of kingship and the reality.

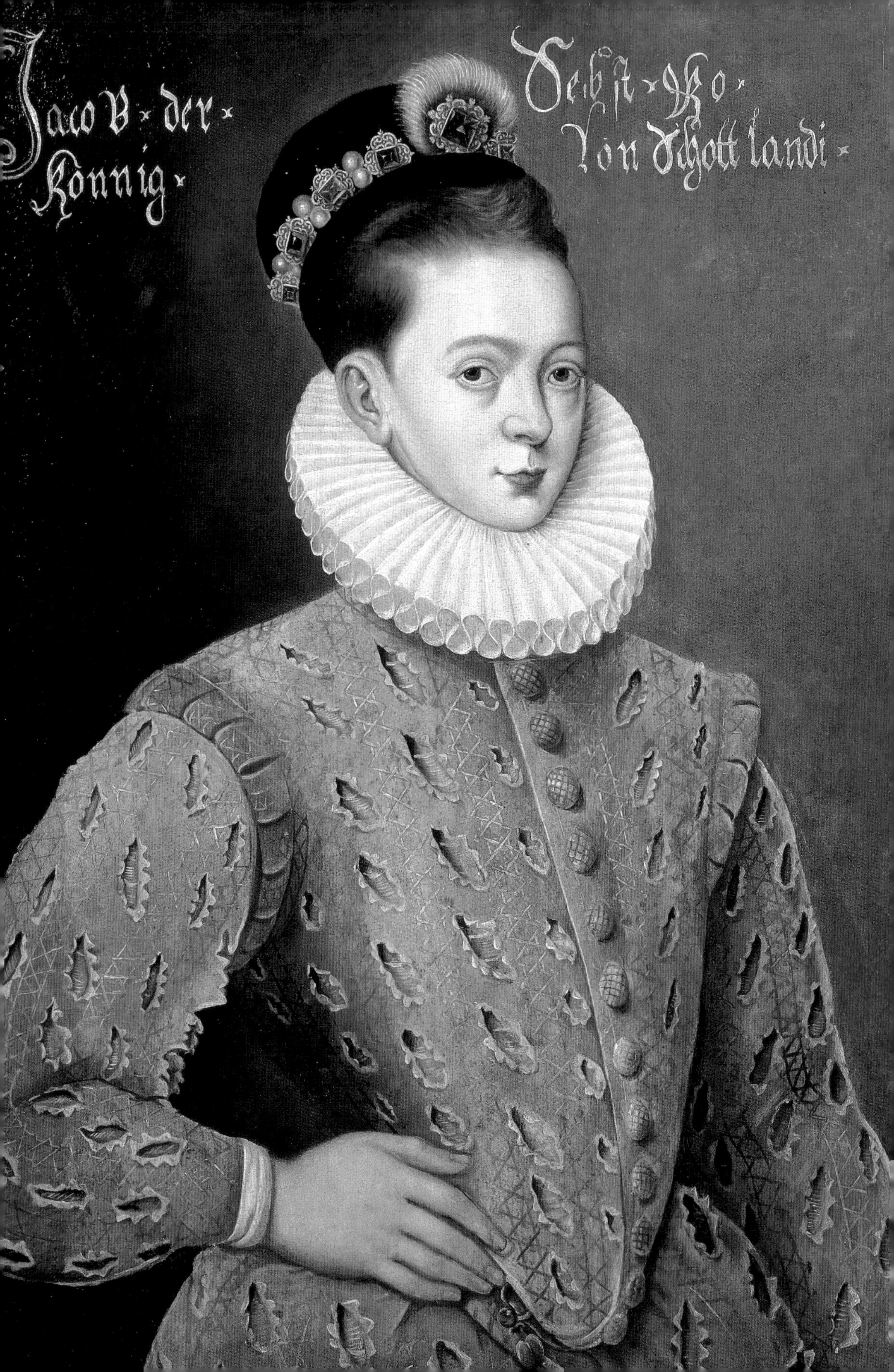
Jaco V der
Konnig
Sebst Ko
Von Schott landi

James VI and I

THE KING OF SCOTS

Despite anxiety and disagreement about the succession in England, which persisted throughout the reign of Elizabeth, and the traditional hostility between England and Scotland, James VI of Scotland claimed the English Crown not as an invader or the puppet of a political faction, but as the rightful heir, almost universally acknowledged. How had this come about, and which aspects of James' Scottish reign had the greatest bearing on his rule in England? James was deeply committed to the creation of a united 'Great Britain', but why did his cherished political union of Scotland and England fail?

James was born on 19 June 1566, in Edinburgh Castle, the son of Mary, Queen of Scots and Henry Stuart, Lord Darnley. With Queen Elizabeth childless and unmarried in England, James was hailed in Scotland as the natural heir to both kingdoms. Despite these great and legitimate hopes he was not born into domestic bliss. His birth came only three months after the murder of Mary's secretary, the Italian David Riccio, by a group of Protestant nobles encouraged by the fervent jealousy of Darnley, who suspected a romantic liaison between them. Henry IV of France, who was fond of a bad joke, said it was right that James was called 'Solomon' since he was the son of David. The suspicion of bastardy hung over James and was a serious enough potential impediment to his claim to the English throne for the Scottish Parliament to pass an Act in 1596, which made it treasonable to slander James' parents. In that year James pressed for Edmund Spenser to be punished in England for passages, said to allude to Mary, in *The Faerie Queene*.

Portrait of James VI of Scotland, attributed to Adrian Vanson. This picture is believed to be the marriage portrait sent to the Danish court as part of James' courtship of his future wife Anne, some four years before they finally married. It was the custom at this time for the European royal families to exchange portraits as the first step in considering potential alliances. Here James appears a pale poetical young man and, initially at least, his love for Anne was expressed in ardent verses.

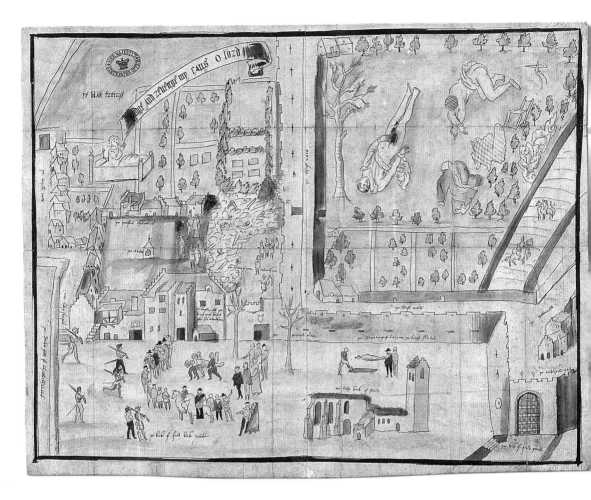

Bird's-eye view of the 'Kirk o' Fields', showing the scene of Darnley's murder, and Darnley's body being borne away and buried. The murder itself is depicted at a larger scale at the top right of the picture. At the top left, the eight-month-old James wakes as from a nightmare or premonition of the murder and (forgetting he is not yet old enough to speak) cries out for vengeance.

In February 1567, Darnley was murdered at his Edinburgh residence Kirk o' Fields; it was widely believed that James Hepburn, Earl of Bothwell was responsible for Darnley's assassination, and Mary was suspected of complicity. Mary not only exonerated Bothwell, but also married him and created him Duke of Orkney, seeming to confirm her guilt. Mary's downfall was swift: that June, abandoned by Bothwell, she was defeated at the Battle of Carberry Hill, and forced to abdicate in favour of her infant son. She escaped imprisonment in Scotland only to find it again in England, where Queen Elizabeth agonized over her fate for the next two decades. Documents relating to these events appear in this series in David Loades' book *Elizabeth I: the golden reign of Gloriana*.

From James' perspective the effects of these events were immediate but also long lasting and profound. He was proclaimed King of Scotland when he was only 13 months old, and though baptized a Catholic he was committed to an impeccably Protestant and somewhat intellectually overwhelming education. His political interests became divorced from those of his Catholic mother. Among his early influences were the reforming theologian John Knox and James' tutor George Buchanan, the statesman, poet and historian, who gave James schooling in practical politics unrivalled in Europe. Both Knox and Buchanan were fiercely critical of Mary, and James found an element of political threat in the humility they urged on the monarchy.

James' attitude to these men and the Protestant nobility who ran Scotland during his minority was mixed. In stark contrast to the Reformation in England, the Reformation in Scotland was carried out in defiance of the monarch. Though James' religious sympathies were with the reformers rather than the Catholics, he came to see the Reformation itself as an act of rebellion.

Stirling Castle, where James was baptized on 17 December 1566, and where he spent much of his childhood. By 1583 the Chapel Royal at Stirling was in a poor state of repair but the birth of Prince Henry in 1594 lent impetus to the building of a new Chapel Royal, which was completed in time for Henry's christening on 30 August. The Union of the Crowns brought about the new Chapel Royal's creation but also led to the decline of the castle. Stirling lost its role as a royal residence, eventually becoming a military base.

Obverse face of a Scottish gold 20 pound piece, 1576. The King holds a sword and olive branch, with the motto *'in utrunque paratus'* or 'skilled in either', the implication being that James was, at the age of 13, already master of the arts of peace and war. Precocious in diplomacy, James showed little appetite for martial pursuits.

Mary was executed on 9 February 1587, after her implication in the Babington Plot. Her death infuriated James, as well as horrifying the Scottish nobility who offered to avenge Mary's death, but in reality James could do little. In 1584 the English Parliament had debarred from the English succession anyone who plotted against Elizabeth, which made it very difficult for James to intercede on his mother's behalf. On a practical level James accepted that his hopes of succession in England required him to abandon his mother to her fate, but there remained resentment and fear, not only on a personal level, but also at the way the monarchy had been treated.

The legacy of these events was a desire for balance, to prevent any one faction in Scotland or in England from growing powerful enough to dictate policy to him. In relation to the English succession this meant that he needed to cultivate sympathy for his claims in both Catholic and Protestant countries abroad while keeping on good terms with Elizabeth. This balancing act earned James a harsh reputation as a dissembler who lacked principle.

Elizabeth could dissemble too and the correspondence between James and the Queen is deeply ambiguous and non-committal on both sides. Elizabeth assured James that though she would not go so far as to name him as her successor, she would do nothing to hinder his claim, 'unless by manifest ingratitude she should be justly moved and provoked to the contrary'. This committed her to nothing and made James subject to her whim.

Increasingly frustrated with Elizabeth's lack of commitment to his succession, not to mention her longevity, James entertained thoughts of invasion with the help of Spain and fantasized about a time when Scotland would be settled, rich and militarily strong enough to invade England unaided. More practically, he sought support from those in England who might induce or compel Elizabeth to name him as her heir. One such was the Earl of Essex, Elizabeth's dashing but ill-fated favourite who, when in favour, appeared to hold the government in his hands. James was too cautious to commit himself inextricably to Essex's abortive rebellion of 9 February 1601, but only just. Read a letter from James to Elizabeth at this time: document 1, *The promised land*.

After the failure of Essex's rebellion James found unexpected support from Robert Cecil, Essex's great enemy at court and, as director of Elizabeth's policy in Scotland, an unpopular man with the Scots and with James himself. Cecil's painstaking preparations before the death of Queen Elizabeth in 1603 are credited for James' virtually unopposed accession to the throne of England. Cecil adopted James for personal reasons as well as reasons of state, calculating that James' peaceable accession would be guaranteed to leave his own power intact, but there were still obstacles to overcome. Lawyers promoting the claim of James' cousin Arabella Stuart argued that as an alien, born in Scotland, James was not entitled to inherit English land. This may help to explain the persistence and tenacity of James' attempts to ask Elizabeth to grant him the estates of his grandparents the Earl and Countess of Lennox.

In the end the English prejudice in favour of a male monarch proved stronger than their prejudice against a Scottish one. Crucially James, who had married in 1589, was not just a man, he was a father of sons. To a nation which had spent much of the previous century agonizing about the succession,

1 The promised land

A two-page letter from James to Queen Elizabeth, written in his own hand on 10 February 1601 – the day after the Earl of Essex's failed rebellion in London, but before news of it reached James in Edinburgh.

In reality the ambassadors James recommends in the letter, Mar and Kinloss, were intended to maintain his contacts with Essex rather than with Elizabeth herself, but by the time James had written the letter the Earl had begun his journey to the Tower and the block. James had considered the popular and powerful Earl an ally in securing his succession and narrowly escaped implication in the rebellion, partly because his written communications with his supporters and the authorities in England were so cautious.

The letter is candid in the sense of admitting past misunderstandings, if putting a favourable gloss on their causes, but it is very wary, a letter to a respected adversary rather than a 'best friend'. It was accompanied by private instructions to his ambassadors to cultivate those favourably inclined to his succession in England while remaining on good terms with the Queen. Three months after this letter promising honesty in his dealings with Elizabeth, James had begun a secret coded correspondence with Robert Cecil, the man Essex had sought to remove from power in his rebellion. The correspondence with Cecil paved the way for James' succession and was conducted without Elizabeth's knowledge. For safety, the principal protagonists were referred to by numbers rather than by their names. Under Cecil's instruction the tone of James' letters to the Queen became noticeably warmer. Mar and Kinloss were two of only a handful of men who knew of the secret correspondence: both were to be made Privy Councillors in England when James came to the throne.

JAMES WROTE:

Madame and dearest sister, As the strait [tight] bonds of our so long continued amity do oblige me, so your daily example used towards me in the like case does invite me not to suffer any misconstrued thoughts against any of your actions to take harbour in my heart but, by laying all my griefs before you, to seek from yourself the right remedy and cure for the same. And since that I have often found by experience that evil-affected or unfit instruments employed between us have oftentimes been the cause of great misunderstanding amongst us, I have therefore at this time made choice of sending to you this nobleman, the Earl of Mar, in respect of his known honesty and constant affection to the continuance of our amity, together with his colleague, the Abbot of Kinloss (a gentleman whose uprightness and honesty is well known to you) that, by the labours of such honest and well-affected ministers, all scruples or griefs may on either side be removed and our constant amity more and more confirmed and made sound. Assuring myself that my ever honest behaviour towards you shall at least procure that justice at your hands to try before you trust any unjust imputations spread of me, and not to wrong yourself in wronging your best friend; but, in respect of the faithfulness of the bearers,

The letter continues:

I will remit all particulars to their relation, as they are dir[ected] to deal with you in all honest plainness (the undisseverable companion of true friendship), so do I heartily pray you to hear and trust them in all things as it were myself and give them a favourable ear and answer as shall ever be deserved at your hands by

Your most loving and affectionate brother and cousin

James R

From Holyrood House the tenth of February 1601

45

11

Madame & dearest sister As the straite bondis of oure so long continued
amitie doe obleishe me so youre daylie example used towardis me in the
lyke caice dois invite me not to suffer any misconstrued thochtis against
any of youre actions to take harboure in my hairt but by laying oppen all
my greifes before you to seeke from youre self the richt remedie &
cure for the same: & since that I have oft founde by experience that
euill affected or unfitt instrumentis emploied betuixt us have often
tymes bene the cause of great misunderstanding amongst us, I have
thairfore at this tyme maid choice of sending unto you this noble man
the erle of marre in respect of his knowin honestie & constant
affection to the continuance of oure amitie together with his collegue
the abbot of kinloffe (a gentleman qchose uprichtnes & honestie is uell
knowin unto you) that by the labouris of suche honest & uell affected ministeris all scrupules or greifis maye on ather syde be removed
& oure constant amitie more & more be confirmed & maid sounde:
assuring my self that my ever honest behavioure towardis you shall at
least procure that iustice at youre handis to trye or ye truste any
iniuste imputations spredd of me, & not to wronge youre self in wronging youre best freind, but in respect of the faithfulnes of the bearar

he brought a dynasty acknowledged to be legitimate even by England's enemies. He had two sons, Henry and Charles (the future Charles I), and a daughter, Elizabeth.

THE KING OF BRITAIN

When Queen Elizabeth died on 24 March 1603 events moved very quickly. Within eight hours James was proclaimed king in London. After years of cloak-and-dagger negotiation James' succession was revealed as government policy. The playwright Thomas Dekker wrote that on Thursday it was treason to say 'God Save King James', on Friday it was high treason not to. Initially the crowds hearing the proclamation were muted and apprehensive. Fear of disorder, even invasion, persisted and the Council closed the ports and imprisoned prominent malcontents. As the disorder failed to materialize, apprehension gave way to relief and then to jubilation. James, who had set off cautiously on his journey south, half expecting to be turned back at Berwick, found himself besieged by English suitors.

A manifesto of the new dynasty from James' own hand arrived in England at the same time as the King himself. In *Basilikon Doron*, a book of instruction to Prince Henry, James counsels him to tell the truth, but adds that 'fair general speeches' are permissible in times of rebellion, a lesson 'Baby Charles' (as the future Charles I was called by his father well into his twenties) would take to heart. *Basilikon Doron* was an instant and enduring publishing success, but there was plenty of competition. If the English were suspicious of the Scots they also became insatiably curious about them. Books and plays about the Scots, exotic and barbarous, abound at this time, the most famous of them being Shakespeare's *Macbeth*.

Basilikon Doron, James' advice to his son on the theory and practice of kingship. For James' critics the chapter headings read like a list of the King's failings: self-love, hypocrisy, lack of judgement in choosing friends and servants, and so on. Certainly Prince Henry is generally held to have been better at living by his father's precepts than the author himself, though Henry's premature death meant he never had the opportunity to do so in power. At first circulated only to a few trusted servants, *Basilikon Doron* gained a long-standing popularity after publication as a source of readily-quotable wisdom.

Against this parochial English view of Scotland James promoted the idea of Britain and a British nation. At the time of his accession there were concerted attempts to show that, far from being a new foreign ruler, James represented the re-establishment of an ancient line of kings. Just as the Normans had used Arthurian romance to establish their connection with a line of 'British' kings before the invading Saxons, James' family tree (see document 2, *A line of Saxon kings*), drawn up at the time, linked him to King Alfred and the Saxon kings who preceded the invading Normans.

Having united the Crowns of England and Scotland, James summoned the English Parliament to pass legislation for the formal political union of the two kingdoms. In an address to Parliament on 19 March 1604 he maintained that

James' pedigree, drawn and dated 26 March 1603, two days after his succession in England. This pedigree, or family tree, of James links him with the ancient British Crown dating back to King Alfred. It was drawn by Robert Bruce Cotton, the famous manuscript collector, to help demonstrate the strength of the new King's claim to the throne and to legitimize the new kingdom of 'Great Britain', which James wanted to create out of the old kingdoms of England and Scotland. The Crown descends via kings whose policies resemble James' own, like the 'peaceful' King Edgar and Alfred himself 'who united the Heptarchy', a king who, like James, brought together a falsely divided realm. Cotton was himself distantly related to Robert the Bruce and was keen to stress his own connections with the new ruling house.

This was all part of the new, foreign regime representing itself as old, established and native, but in truth the strength of James' claim lay not in the blood of his ancestors but the political stability offered by his descendants. James' dynasty survived in a way no one could have anticipated. Prince Henry died of typhoid in 1612 and Charles was executed in 1649. Princess Elizabeth provided the enduring link to the modern monarchy after the death of Queen Anne. The house of Hanover descended from Elizabeth's daughter Sophia, whose son became George I. It has been said that one of the illnesses from which James appears to have suffered was porphyria and that he introduced it into the English royal family. This malady is thought to have been responsible for the 'madness' of King George III.

THE FAMILY TREE READS:

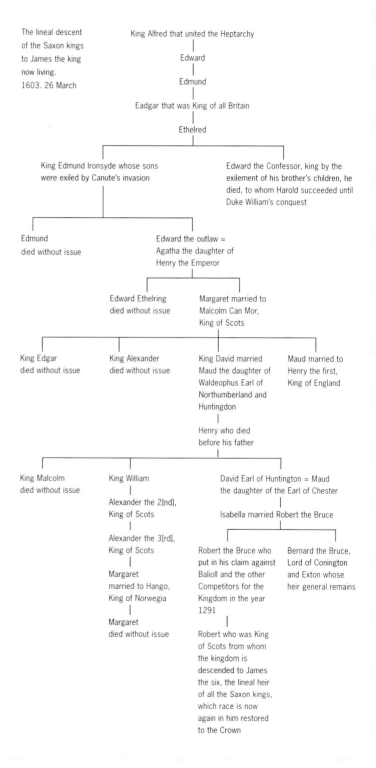

The lineal descent of the Saxon kings to James the king now living. 1603. 26 March

King Alfred that united the Heptarchy
|
Edward
|
Edmund
|
Eadgar that was King of all Britain
|
Ethelred

King Edmund Ironsyde whose sons were exiled by Canute's invasion

Edward the Confessor, king by the exilement of his brother's children, he died, to whom Harold succeeded until Duke William's conquest

Edmund died without issue

Edward the outlaw = Agatha the daughter of Henry the Emperor

Edward Ethelring died without issue

Margaret married to Malcolm Can Mor, King of Scots

King Edgar died without issue

King Alexander died without issue

King David married Maud the daughter of Waldeophus Earl of Northumberland and Huntingdon
|
Henry who died before his father

Maud married to Henry the first, King of England

King Malcolm died without issue

King William
|
Alexander the 2nd, King of Scots
|
Alexander the 3rd, King of Scots
|
Margaret married to Hango, King of Norwegia
|
Margaret died without issue

David Earl of Huntington = Maud the daughter of the Earl of Chester
|
Isabella married Robert the Bruce

Robert the Bruce who put in his claim against Balioll and the other Competitors for the Kingdom in the year 1291
|
Robert who was King of Scots from whom the kingdom is descended to James the six, the lineal heir of all the Saxon kings, which race is now again in him restored to the Crown

Bernard the Bruce, Lord of Conington and Exton whose heir general remains

the lineall dessent of the
Saxon kings to James
the king now liuing
1603. 26. March.

King Alfred that vnited
the Heptarchy

Edward

Eadmund

Eadgar that was
totius Britaniæ
Basileus

Æthelred

king Edmund Jronsyde
whos sonnes wear
exiled by Canutus
inuasion

Edward the Confessor king by
the exilment of his brother
children he died, to whom
Harold succeded vntill Duk
william conquest

Edmund
sine prole

Edward the
out lawe

Agatha the
daughter of
Hen: the 2
Emperor

Edward
Ethelring
sine prole

Margaret
maried to

Malcolme
Canmor
king of scotts

King Edgar
sine prole

king Alexander
sine prole

king Dauid
maried

Maud the daughter of
waldeophus Erle of
Northumberland and
Huntingdon

Maud maried to
Henry the first
King of England

Henry who
died before
his father

king Malcolme
sine prole

king william

Dauid Earl of
Huntington

Maud the daughter
of the Earl of Chester

Alexander
the 2 king
of scotts

Isabella maried
to Robert de
Brus

Alexander 3
King of scotts

Robert de Brus
who put in his claim
against Balioll and
the other Competitors
for the Kingdom
a.º 1291

Bernard de Brus
dominus de Conington
et Exton whos heir
generall remaineth

Margaret maried
to Hango King
of Nerwegia

Margarett
sine prole

Robert who
was king of
Scotts from whom
the kingdom is
dessended to James
the six the lineall
heir of all the Saxon
kings which race is
now agayn in him restored
to the Crowne

Britain was a governable entity, which had been artificially divided but which could be reunited. James styled himself the Husband of Britain, who could not therefore be expected to have two wives (Scotland and England). In saying this he was making a political point but he was also emphasizing his role as family man, capitalizing on the favourable moral impression he had made by his apparent lack of sexual interest in women other than his wife Anne. Here, as one of his bishops remarked, James was superior to Solomon.

Papered impression of the smaller of the two signets described in document 3, showing a shield of the royal arms between the initials J R [*Jacobus Rex*]. James could credibly claim kingship of England and Scotland and Ireland. Any formal claim to the throne of France had been renounced in Elizabeth's reign but the monarchy retained the title of ruler of 'England, Scotland, France and Ireland' long afterwards.

Parliament was unenthusiastic about the union and fearful of a Scottish take-over. There was an element of xenophobia in this, because although there had been an influx of Scots into the government, a natural consequence of the dissolution of the Scottish royal court, only a very few had been appointed to the most important positions. A commission was set up to investigate the political union of the two countries and a whole volume of State Papers is devoted to the articles of the proposed union, but the project died in legal wrangling. James was frustrated at Parliament's lack of vision and the slowness with which it acted. He became suspicious of the English common lawyers who hid their prejudice behind nice legal points.

Though no formal union could take place without Parliament, James did what he could by other means. Just as Henry VII had united

The Somerset House conference of 1604, by Pantonia de la Cruz. This group portrait commemorates the peace treaty between England and Spain, ending a war which had dragged on since the Armada. Second from the window on the right is Charles Howard, Earl of Nottingham who, as Elizabeth's Lord Admiral, had defeated the Spanish in 1588. James' policy towards Spain now centred on negotiations for a marriage treaty for Prince Henry and later for Prince Charles with a Spanish princess. Between 20 May and 16 July 1604, 18 conference sessions were held at Somerset House, and the treaty was signed on 16 August.

Shakespeare's company of actors, The King's Men, were paid for their attendance from 9–27 August, which suggests they were there as part of celebrations either side of the signing when the negotiations were safely concluded.

the houses of York and Lancaster in the Tudor Rose, James wanted a new symbol of the united kingdoms of England and Scotland. Read a royal warrant for Britain's new emblem: document 3, *Union of the Crowns*.

James was also determined to reunite his English Privy Council, which had descended into political faction in the final years of Elizabeth. The failure and ignominy of the Essex rebellion had left Robert Cecil dominant in the Council, but though he had followed Cecil's instructions faithfully to secure his crown James was not to be Cecil's puppet now he wore it. James rehabilitated members of the Earl of Essex's former party and of the Catholic Howard family who had opposed the execution of his mother, Mary Queen of Scots. This has been seen as a retrospective attempt to reward those who had opposed Elizabeth's policy. James was not one to condone or reward rebellion against Princes, even those he disliked, and it is possible to see his broadening of the Council as an attempt to heal rifts among the nobility and restore the balance of power.

3 *Union of the Crowns*

A warrant (shown in the middle section of the page), dated 4 April 1603, to the royal engraver Charles Anthony to make two signets combining the arms of England and Scotland. Robert Cecil issued this warrant while the King himself was still in Edinburgh. Though the new signets symbolized the union of the Scottish and English Crowns, real political union of the two kingdoms proved more difficult to achieve thanks to the scepticism of the English Parliament.

The union of England and Scotland was a personal crusade for James who did as much as he could by royal warrant and decree to bring it about since he could not do so by legislation through Parliament. Fittingly the signet itself, as the personal seal of the monarch, was an instrument of this personal legislation.

Its use had become an established part of the process of government and was seen as unobjectionable in times of trust between the monarch and the political establishment. Overuse of the signet when such trust was absent could be interpreted as the monarch taking too much power, a sign of incipient tyranny. The battle with Parliament over the union was an early sign that James and his successors would have increasing recourse to personal legislation without Parliament.

Not least among the advantages of full union anticipated by James would be an end to the raids and general lawlessness in the border country, crime which exploited the separate jurisdictions of England and Scotland. James saw this area as the midlands of his new kingdom,

peaceable and industrious. The raids continued as a constant reminder of the failure of the union and James attempted to deal severely with the perpetrators.

Ironically, formal political union only came about by the Act of Union in 1707, which was partly designed to stop James' direct descendants being proclaimed kings of Scotland. Without full union, the Scots might proclaim their own Catholic Stuart king, even though the English Parliament had settled both kingdoms on the Protestant House of Hanover. This new ruling dynasty, which came to power in 1714 after the death of Queen Anne, traced its own descent from the Electress Sophia, who was James' grand-daughter (see p. 109).

THE WARRANT READS:

Warrant for the new making of the signets:

Whereas the King's majesty has of late signified his pleasure to me Robert Cecil, knight, his majesty's principal Secretary for order to be taken for new Signets to be made for the sealing of his majesty's letters and other warrants in such sort as it is fit the said seals should now be made with the union of the Arms of both Realms England and Scotland, with the which his majesty's pleasure in that behalf we having been made acquainted and thereon considered of the order for the placing of the said Arms, these are now to will and command you with all expedition [speed] to make two Signets of such gold as has been heretofore [before now] accustomed one greater [larger] and one lesser [smaller] and to be graven [engraved] according to these patterns delivered to you and with these circumscriptions [inscriptions around the edge] and the same so made to be brought and delivered to the said Robert Cecil to remain with him to be used for the service of his majesty as aforesaid. And allowance shall be made to you for the gold and workmanship according as it shall appear by former precedence has been allowed.

And these shall be unto [for] you sufficient warrant and discharge in that behalf. From the King's majesty's palace of Whitehall the fourth of April 1603.

About your greater Seal:

[In Latin] James, by the grace of God, King of England, Scotland, France and Ireland, defender of the faith.

About your lesser Seal:

[In Latin] James, by the grace of God, King of England, Scotland, France and Ireland.

To Charles Anthony his Majesty's [en]graver for his Seals and Stamps.

route and crimes and those committed in my jeofferme whereto the Justices of assise over and determiner cannot conveniently be sent from Dublin to heare all offerances and complaints of the people residing in those parts, and sumarily without judiciall or formall proceeding in lawlike manner to ende and right the same tending to Justice as well in criminall causes as in controversies betweene partie and partie, so far forth as the want of Comitie grounde or Juries for trialls or the barbarousnes of those vnciuill people be no impediment, but y each of this libertie in those parts may remaine hope to be righted in all iust causes by the ciuill Justice and by the authoritie marshall in such maner as you with the advise of some of the priuie Counsell and Counsell learned there shall thinke most expedient.

A warrant for new making of the Signetts

Cal.
4 Aprl 1603

The kings Matie hath of late signified his pleasure vnto me Robt Cecill knight his Maties principall Secretarie for order to be taken for new Cignette to be made for the sealing of his Maties grantes and other warrants in such sorte as it is fitt the said Seales should now be made with the armes of the armes of both Realmes England and Scotland, of the which his Maties pleasure in that behalf we hauing bene made acquainted and thereon considered of the order for the placing of the said Armes, these are now to will and commaunde you with all expedition to make two Signetts of fyne gold as hath bene heretofore accustomed one greater and one lesser and to be grauen according to these patternes deliuered vnto you, and with these armes, inscriptions and the same so made to be brought and deliuered to the said Robt Cecill to remaine with him to be vsed for the seruice of his Matie as aforesaid. And allowance shall be made vnto you for the gold and workmanshipp according as it shall happen to be by former presidents to haue bene allowed. And these shall be vnto you sufficient warrant and discharge in that behalf. from the kings Matie pallace of Westehall the fourth of Aprill 1603.

About the greater Seale

Jacobus D: G: Ang: Sco: fran: et Hib: Rex: fid: def:

About the lesser Seale.

Jacobus D: G: Ang: Sco: fran: et Hib: Rex.

Charles Anthony his Maties grauer for his Seales and Stamps.

A Comission to the L. L. Admirall & y Earle of Worcester to execute y office of Earle Marshall

Cal Dom
1601 Dec 10

Elizabeth by the grace of God &c. To the right trusty and welbeloued Counsellor Thomas Lo: Burrhurst o' high Treasorer of England and to the right trusty and right welbeloued Cousins and Counsellors Charles Earle of Nottingham o' high Admirall of England and Edward Earle of Worcester master of o' horse greeting. Whereas the office of the Earle marshall of this o' Realme of England is voyde by the attainder of the late Earle of Essex, and by reason thereof vntill we shall dispose of the same office to some person if you meete for yt there are and wilbe many incidents of Armes & Chiualry belonging to the same office, vndetermined and of late growne for want of due regarde had to the actions of officers the Heralds and kings of Armes and pursuants of Armes, we are informed that diuers euills are committed by certaine Heralds now deceased & by some such as doo now liue to the dishonor of o' nobilitie, and Chiualrye and to the disgrace of sondry families of ancient blood bearing the Armes of their Aunistors in assigning and appointing the ancient Armes badges & Crests of some of the nobilitie and Chiualrie, and of other gentlemen of ancient blood to men that were and yet be strangers in blood & not inheritable thereto. And likewise for game or other affection the said Heralds haue appointed Armes Crests and badges for some other persons of base birth or of meane alteration & qualitie of liuing, that were meete for persons of good birth & lignage, to receiue some ...

Portrait of Shakespeare discovered in Venice and inscribed in Italian '*Scoti Lanza*: ['Shake spear'], English playwright 21 July 1604'. The portrait might possibly have come to Venice via the Venetian Embassy in London. This portrait, unlike some contemporary likenesses, bears a strong resemblance to the Shakespeare of the Stratford memorial. Many of the playwrights of the age seemed to lead a double life, as royal servants entertaining the court in the masque and as writers for the public stages risking the displeasure of the Privy Council by commenting on the affairs of state. Shakespeare seems to have escaped censure though his company had to talk their way out of a tight corner when they undertook a special performance of *Richard II* on the eve of the Essex rebellion.

The Privy Council expanded from 12 to 35 members. This has been seen as part of James' famous (or infamous) profligacy in bestowing honours, but in fact expansion was necessary. Elizabeth had been slow to grant honours and replace councillors so that with death and disfavour her circle of advisers narrowed and their individual influence increased.

James' determination to confirm existing officials in their places and privileges, and to add to them, extended to the acting companies. On 17 May 1603 he issued a warrant for letters patent for Shakespeare's company to continue playing 'for the recreation of the king's loving subjects and for his own solace and pleasure when he shall think good to see them'. Though James had been crowned in England in July 1603, the usual processions and celebrations had not taken place because, at the time, the plague was raging in London. James himself had taken refuge at Wilton where Shakespeare's company performed a play thought to be *As You Like It*. Over the Christmas celebrations 1603–4, 30 plays and masques were performed at court, the most important being a masque before the Spanish ambassador, which presaged a treaty with Spain. The coronation progress through London finally took place in March 1604, when the actors were listed in their new role as royal servants (see document 4, *Shakespeare, the King's Man*).

The accounts of the Master of the Revels for court performances in 1605. The Master of the Revels was the official responsible for plays and masques at court and issuing licences for public theatre. This is a rare official record of Shakespeare as playwright 'the poet that made the play' rather than as an actor. The authenticity of the record was disputed but has since been established.

4 *Shakespeare, the King's Man*

An entry from the account book of the royal progress through the city of London, 15 March 1604.

James' coronation in plague-stricken London in July 1603 had been shorn of much of the usual pageant and procession because of the fear of great crowds spreading the disease. Finally, in March 1604, the processions took place. This account book records the amounts of cloth given to nearly 1,100 royal servants to make the livery in which to attend the occasion.

The three principal dramatic companies, The King's, Queen's and Prince Henry's Men are all represented in the account book. This entry features The King's Men including Shakespeare himself, as well as Hemmings and Condell who were responsible for collecting and preserving his plays for the First Folio edition, and the principal actors Burbage and Armyn. As well as the procession itself there were pageants at which the players were prominent.

The close direct relationship between the acting companies and the Crown is indicated by the fact that expenses for their services are paid for out of the personal accounts of their patrons in the way fools and jesters had traditionally been.

Shakespeare's company seems to have been in attendance on the Spanish ambassadors at Somerset House at the time of the negotiation of the Spanish Treaty in August 1604. An Audit Office account, preserved in the National Archives, records 'To Augustine Phillippes and John Hemynges for the allowance of themselves and ten of their fellows his Majesty's grooms of the chamber and Players for waiting and attending on his Majesty's service by commandment upon the Spanish ambassador at Somerset House the space of 18 days viz from the 9th day of August until the 27th day of the same as appears by a bill thereof signed by the Lord Chamberlain £21 12s'. This was good money but to judge by the portrait (p.15) of the assembled ambassadors, which commemorated the occasion, they were a tough crowd to entertain.

THE ACCOUNT BOOK ENTRY FOR THE KING'S MEN READS:

	William Shakespeare	4.5 yards
	Augustine Phillipps	4.5 yards
	Lawrence Fletcher	4.5 yards
	John Hemming[es]	4.5 yards
Players	Richard Burbidge	4.5 yards

Damask Scarlet, Red Cloth

William Slye	4.5 yards
Robert Armyn	4.5 yards
Henry Cundell	4.5 yards
Richard Cowley	4.5 yards

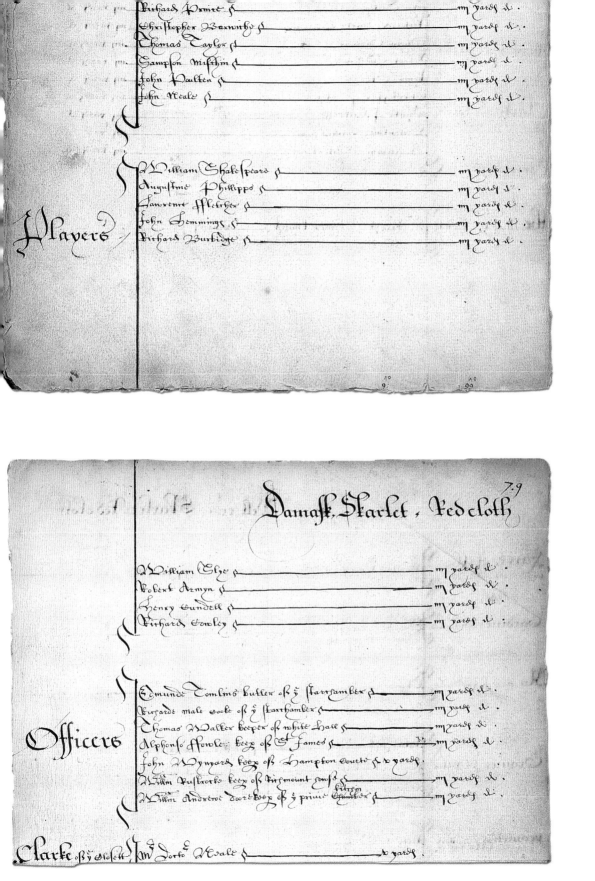

Richard Ormer   iij yards di.
Christopher Baxwith   iij yards di.
Thomas Tayler   iij yards di.
Sampson Misthin   iij yards di.
John Paulten   iij yards di.
John Neale   iij yards di.

Players
William Shakespeare   iij yards di.
Augustine Phillipps   iij yards di.
Lawrence Fletcher   iij yards di.
John Hemminges   iij yards di.
Richard Burbidge   iij yards di.

Damask, Scarlet, Red cloth

William Slye   iij yards di.
Robert Armyn   iij yards di.
Henry Cundell   iij yards di.
Richard Cowley   iij yards di.

Officers
Edmunde Tomlins butler of ye Starrchamber   iij yards di.
Richard Male cooke of ye Starrchamber   iij yards di.
Thomas Walker keeper of white hall   iij yards di.
Alphonso Fowle keep of St James   iij yards di.
John Wynyard keep of Hampton Courte   iij yards.
Willm Bustroke keep of Richmount house   iij yards di.
Willm Andrewe doore keep of ye privie Chamber   iij yards di.

Clarke of ye Closet Mr Doctor Neale   x yards.

The Bible and Witchcraft

THE KING JAMES BIBLE

The King James Bible or Authorized Version had its origins in a conference at Hampton Court in 1604 intended to unify the English Church. In the same year Parliament passed a new Witchcraft Act. Both have been closely associated with James himself. What role did the translation play in James' religious policy and to what extent was it the King's personal project? Was the Witchcraft Act an attempt by James the witch-hunter to impose his peculiar obsessions on his new kingdom? What was the true nature of James' famous fascination with witches and how did he act in cases concerning them?

Window portrait of James, reputedly from Wroxton Abbey, Oxfordshire. This portrait, though formal in its setting, shows something of James' character. He appears impatient with his pose, even argumentative, ready to brandish his sceptre, perhaps to emphasize some minor theological point. The window may be the work of Abraham van Linge who worked on the chapel at Wroxton and later on the enamelled glass of the chapel of Lincoln College, Oxford, where Adam is depicted bearing a marked resemblance to Charles I.

James had moved quickly to broaden his Privy Council, balancing the factions within it and, through the treaty with Spain, to redress the balance in English foreign policy, which had become fervently anti-Spanish in the last years of Elizabeth. James also sought to pursue a balanced religious policy. In practice this meant that Puritans and Catholics alike were obliged to conform, at least outwardly, alongside a broad Anglican Church under James' authority and controlled by his bishops. James interpreted any failure to outwardly conform as a challenge to royal authority, but within the Church his appointments reflected a broad spectrum of theological opinion.

The idea for the Hampton Court conference came from the Puritans. Their 'Millenary Petition', presented to James on his progress south, was a moderate and respectful plea for reform of the Church and was well received by the King. By the time of the conference itself in January 1604, James, advised by his bishops,

Hampton Court palace. Like Henry VIII, the monarch most associated with the palace, James loved Hampton Court for the excellent hunting in the park. For James it was a genuine home, a place of rest and recreation, hosting festivities and theatricals as well as being a venue for formal business. That the conference was held here reflected not only James' role as head of the English Church, but also his personal interest in its proceedings and his attempt to engage on a more informal basis with theologians, as he had done with the Kirk in Scotland.

had come to suspect that the Puritans aimed at a system of Church government without bishops or the King similar to the one he disliked so much in Scotland. The first day of the conference was reserved for bishops and privy councillors to set the agenda. When the debate began openly, some bishops were surprised and alarmed at the King's willingness to entertain Puritan opinion, but it was soon clear that James' aim was to drive a wedge between moderate and radical Puritans, inviting the former into the established Church and suppressing the latter.

Dr John Reynolds was prominent among the Puritan delegates. He suggested a new translation of the Bible and became one of the project's leading lights. A chance remark by Reynolds seemed to confirm James' fears about Puritan designs on the government of the Church; James insulted him roundly, but the idea of the new Bible persisted. This was partly because James had himself urged a new translation on the Kirk in Scotland in 1601. There, as in England, the popular Bible was the Geneva version with its topical marginal notes, which made it, in James' eyes, an anti-monarchical handbook of revolution. The approved English Bible, the so-called 'Bishops' Bible' was remote and unpopular. The new version was to bridge the gap between the two by being approved, authoritative and popular. James determined that the most learned and able translators should be chosen for the work, which should then be officially approved by submission to the Council and ratified by royal authority. Read document 5, *The royal Bible*, concerning the Bible translators.

The King James Bible or Authorized Version. Translating the Bible into English had always been a political act. In his Easter Day sermon of 1622 the poet John Donne, then a royal chaplain, reminded James that even monarchs could not hope to monopolize God's political backing despite claims made at the time of the Armada or the Gunpowder Plot. 'Our God is not out of breath, because he has blown one tempest, and swallowed a Navy: our God has not burnt out his eyes, because he has looked upon a Train of Powder.'

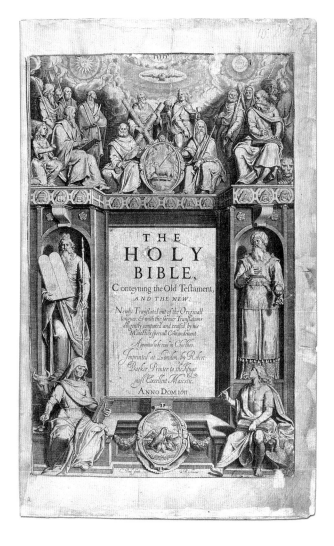

The translators selected by the King's criteria were organized into groups or companies, with each chapter being cross checked and difficult points discussed. They were also instructed to follow the 'Bishops' Bible' where possible, rendering keywords conservatively like 'church' rather than 'congregation'.

In the event the 'Bishops' Bible' played only a very small part in the final version, and the new translation itself took material from a range of earlier bibles. Like the Geneva, the Authorized Version owed most to William Tyndale, who had embarked on a translation of the Bible a century earlier, but had been executed for his pains in 1536. This time, though, the political approach of the appointed translators, outlined in their Preface, owed more to James than to Tyndale. In the previous century, arguing against critics who said English was too 'rough' to translate the subtle meanings of the original languages, Tyndale had countered that the Greek and especially Hebrew agreed so closely with English that a translation almost syllable for syllable

5 The royal Bible

A warrant, dated 22 July 1604, specifying the contents of a letter to be sent to the Bishop of London. The Bishop is being asked to recommend the translators of the King James Bible for any church posts which become vacant, in order to provide them with additional income. He is also asked to seek out scholars in Greek and Hebrew.

James' most successful personal project was the Bible bearing his name. Unlike so many official appointments in the reign, the appointment of translators was done on merit, though James was keen to bring such scholars into his patronage by engineering clerical livings for them. James had tried other means to fund the project including asking the bishops to contribute funds, but this had not gained the bishops' wholehearted support.

Bishop Bancroft, who had disagreed with the promoters of the new translation at Hampton Court, became Archbishop of Canterbury soon afterwards and thereby became the overseer of the project and, as the authors of the Preface to the translation put it, its 'taskmaster'. Bancroft has been accused of making a number of changes to the translation to suit his own view of Church government. Bancroft had shown practical loyalty to Queen Elizabeth by raising a body of pikemen to help put down the Essex rebellion. His continued rise under James perhaps proved that loyalty to the Crown earned James' approbation more than mere actions in his interest.

The 54 translators mentioned here were divided into six groups or companies, two at Westminster under the direction of Lancelot Andrewes, two at Oxford under John Harding and two at Cambridge under Edward Lively. Both Harding and Lively were professors of Hebrew, Harding being gradually eclipsed as the driving force of the Oxford group by John Reynolds, who had disputed with James at Hampton Court. Andrewes was one of the breed of clergymen James most admired, mixing piety with social polish, learning with wit. Many historians have judged him harshly for giving his consent to the Essex divorce (see Chapter 4, The British Solomon).

A letter to the Bishop of London that whereas his majesty has appointed 54 learned men for the translating of the Bible (whereof divers [many] of them have not [got] preferment worthy their deserts) that in his majesty's name he write to the Archbishop of York and the rest of the Bishops in the Province of Canterbury, it is his majesty's pleasure when any prebend or parsonage of the yearly rent of twenty pounds or upwards shall be void either of their gift or of any other parsons, that they do stay [delay] the admittance to them, till his majesty may commend for the same some of the said learned men, [and] that they do inform themselves of such as are learned in the Hebrew and Greek tongues and have taken pains for clearing of any obscurities in the Scriptures and that they send their observations to Mr Lively or Dr Harding or Dr Andrewes to be imparted to the rest. Dated at Westminster the 22nd of July 1604. Perused by the Lord Bishop of London.

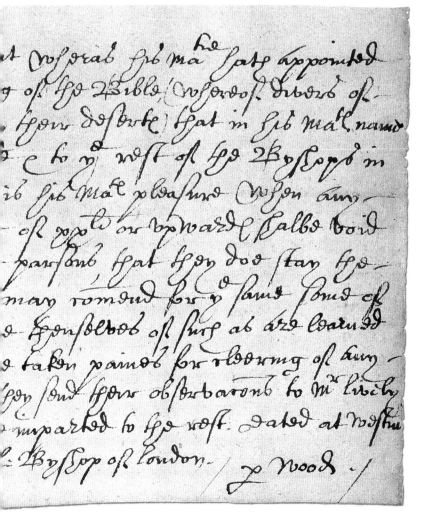

would be direct, straightforward and comprehensible to the ploughboy. The new translators saw a direct translation of the ancient and mysterious originals as a way of deepening appreciation of that mystery. Ironically Tyndale's language aided the translators in this, for in the intervening years English had acquired, through loan words and new coinages, a sophisticated, wider vocabulary. Tyndale's language no longer spoke directly to the reader as it had done in the 1530s but already sounded rather antique; authoritative but not topical, rather in the way it strikes the modern reader. The Authorized Version sounded old-fashioned when it was published and deliberately so.

The marginal notes of the Geneva Bible, which not only supplied political parallels but encouraged readers to supply their own, were firmly ejected, and the general effect of the new version was that it should appear clear and definitive but mysterious, so that the Bible was no longer a handbook of revolution but a glimpse of divine authority mediated though James himself.

Anne of Denmark in 1617, two years before her death. James did not entrust Prince Henry's upbringing to her which led to a violent quarrel and, it is commonly supposed, a miscarriage. Though his marriage had forged a Protestant alliance with the house of Denmark, Anne became Catholic in the 1590s and refused to take Anglican Communion at James' coronation. Anne devoted herself to court entertainments, spending extravagantly on the production of masques, including Jonson's *Masque of Blackness* which caused consternation among courtiers for the scantness of the costume she and her fellow masquers wore. Her London home, Denmark House, became a centre of artistic life. She shared James' love of hunting with dogs, but shot his favourite dog accidentally.

WITCHCRAFT

To James, witchcraft was a branch of theology and he frequently drew parallels between the two. He considered that there were more female witches than there were male sorcerers because Satan had seduced Eve and had a closer relationship with that sex. His views on witchcraft had been expressed at length in

his treatise *Daemonologie*, published in 1597. In this work his ideas, though largely conventional, were vividly expressed and he described in detail the appearance of demons and devils.

The 1604 Witchcraft Act added to existing legislation, making it a capital offence to cause injury to human beings or damage to property by conjuration. It also made some particular and ghoulish enhancements, which seem to have their origins in James' experience of treasonable witchcraft in Scotland. Read an extract from the Witchcraft Act of 1604, document 6, *A law for witches*.

In 1589 tempestuous seas had prevented James' bride, Anne of Denmark, from sailing to Scotland to meet him. The Danish Admiral blamed the storms on witches in Copenhagen. Anne had got as far as Oslo, but after months in which she failed to arrive and no ships being able to bring news, James set out from Scotland to collect her (for her safety, the Scottish councillors with the Queen had not wished her to return all the way to Copenhagen).

A woodcut depicting tempestuous seas and the now traditional cauldron, from *Newes from Scotland*. Dr Fian, the schoolmaster shown here, had the misfortune to have his failure to confess under torture recorded as a sure sign of guilt 'notwithstanding all the grievous pains and cruel torments he would not confess anything, so deeply had the Devil entered into his heart'. The learned judges do not seem to have been troubled that both confessing and failing to confess could be taken as sure signs of guilt. Dr Fian was burned on Castle Hill in Edinburgh in January 1591.

6 *A law for witches*

An extract from the Chancery enrolment of the Witchcraft Act of 1604. This highly controversial piece of legislation has been cited as evidence that James was a witch-hunter. It adds offences to the witchcraft Acts passed under Elizabeth, and is in some ways more severe in its punishments, but the additions are quite specific, possibly reflecting James' reaction to the treasonable witchcraft practised at North Berwick. There is other evidence which suggests that legislation was being considered before James' accession and that it may not be as personal to James as is often assumed.

There is no question about the government's belief in witchcraft. There is no suggestion of pretence or simulation about offences detailed here. It is clear that the government believed that it was possible to cause harm at a distance with body parts and that evil and wicked spirits could be and were summoned and used. This, at least in part, was because of the link between demonology and theology. Not to believe in evil spirits suggested scepticism about good ones, which bordered on atheism.

James' practical approach to cases brought under this Act is shown to be complex and in many cases sceptical.

He gained a reputation as an uncoverer of witchcraft fraud, in the Haydock and Gunter cases (see document 7) and in a notable episode in Leicestershire, in 1616, when he saved five witches convicted under this legislation on the evidence of a boy of about 12 years old who simulated possession. He was too late to save nine others already convicted and lectured the judges on their gullibility. Official horror at witchcraft and conjuration certainly existed, but that did not prevent the authorities from taking advice from the notorious necromancer Simon Forman in seeking to trace the Gunpowder Plotters.

THE ACT READS:

Be it enacted by the King, our sovereign lord, the Lords spiritual and temporal, and the Commons in this present Parliament assembled, and by the authority of the same, that the statute made in the fifth year of the reign of our late sovereign Lady of most famous and happy memory. Queen Elizabeth intituled [entitled] 'An Act against conjurations, enchantments, and witchcrafts' be from the Feast of Saint Michael the Archangel next coming, for and concerning all offences to be committed after the same feast, utterly repealed.

And for the better restraining the said offences, and more severe punishing the same, be it further enacted by the authority aforesaid, that if any person or persons, after the said Feast of Saint Michael the Archangel next coming, [a] shall use, practice, or exercise any invocation, or conjuration, of any evil and wicked spirit, or shall consult, covenant with, entertain, employ, feed, or reward any evil and wicked spirit to or for any intent or purpose; or [b] take up any dead man, woman, or child out of his, her, or their grave, or any other place where the dead body rests, or the skin, bone, or any other part of any dead person, to be employed or used in any manner of witchcraft, sorcery, charm, or enchantment; or [c] shall use, practise, or exercise any witchcraft, enchantment, charm, or sorcery, whereby any person shall be killed, destroyed, wasted, consumed, pined [wasted by suffering or hunger], or lamed in his or her body, or any part thereof; that then every such offender or offenders,

their aiders, abettors, and counsellors, being of any the said offences duly and lawfully convicted and attainted, shall suffer pains of death as a felon or felons, and shall lose the privilege and benefit of clergy and sanctuary.

And further, to the intent that all manner of practice, use, or exercise of witchcraft, enchantment, charm, or sorcery should be from henceforth utterly avoided, abolished, and taken away, be it enacted by the authority of this present Parliament, that if any person or persons shall, from and after the said Feast of Saint Michael the Archangel next coming, take upon him or them by witchcraft, enchantment, charm, or sorcery, [a] to tell or declare in what place any treasure of gold or silver should or might be found or had in the earth or other secret places, or where goods or things lost or stolen should be found or become; or [b] to the intent to provoke any person to unlawful love; or [c] whereby any chattel or goods of any person shall be destroyed, wasted, or impaired; or [d] to hurt or destroy any person in his or her body, although the same be not effected and done; that then all and every such person and persons so offending, and being thereof lawfully convicted, shall for the said offence suffer imprisonment by the space of one whole year, without bail or mainprise [surety], and once in every quarter of the said year shall in some market town, upon the market day or at such time as any fair shall be kept there, stand openly upon the pillory by the space of six hours, and there shall openly confess his or her error and offence…

Be it enacted by the kinge our Soueraigne lorde, the lordes
Spirituall and Temporall and the Comons in this present Parliament assembled
and by the authoritie of the same that the Statute made in the fifte yere
of the Raigne of our late Soueraigne ladie of famous and happie memorie
Queene Elizabeth intituled An Acte againste Coniurationes Inchauntmentes and
Witchcraftes be from the feaste of St Michaell the Archangell next cominge,
for and touchinge all offences to be committed after the same ffeaste vtterlie
repealed. And for the better restrayninge the saide offences and more seuere
punishinge the same, Be it further enacted by the authoritie aforesaide, That
if any person or persons after the saide ffeaste of St Michaell the Archangell
next cominge shall vse practise or exercise any Inuocation, Coniuration of any
euill and wicked Spirit or shall consult couenant with entertaine employ feede
or rewarde any euill and wicked Spirit, to or for any intent or purpose or take vp
any dead man woman or child out of his her or theire graue or any other place
where the dead bodie resteth, or the skin bone or any other parte of any dead
person, to be imployed or vsed in any manner of Witchcrafte Sorcerie charme or
inchantment, or shall vse practise or exercise any Witchcrafte Inchantment
Charme or Sorcerie wherebie any person shalbe killed, destroyed wasted or
consumed pined or lamed in his or her bodie, or any parte thereof: That then
euerie such offendor or offendors their Aydors abettors and Counsellors
beinge of any the saide offences dulie and lawfullie conuicted and attainted
shall suffer paines of deathe, as a felon or felons, and shall loose the
priuiledge and benefit of Cleargie and Sanctuarie.

And further to the intent that all manner of practise vse or exercise of
Witchcrafte Enchantment Charme or Sorcerie should be from henceforth
vtterlie auoyded abolished, and taken awaye; Be it enacted by the authoritie
of this present Parliament, That if any person or persons shall from and after the
saide ffeaste of Sainct Michaell the Archangell next cominge, take vpon him
or them by Witchcrafte Inchantment Charme, or Sorcerie to tell or declare,
in what place any Treasure of Golde, or Siluer should or might be founde
or had in the earth, or other secret places, or where goodes or thinges loste or
stollen should be founde or become, or to the intent to prouoke any person to
vnlawfull loue, or whereby any Cattell or Goods of any person shalbe destroyed
wasted or impaired, or to hurte or destroy any person in his or her bodie although
the same be not effected and done; That then all and euerie such person or
persons so offendinge, and beinge thereof lawfullie conuicted shall for the saide
offence suffer imprisonment by the space of one whole yere without
baile or mainprise, and once in euerie quarter of the saide yere, shall in some
markett Towne vpon the markett day, or at such tyme as any faire shalbe
kepte, there stande openlie vpon the Pillorie by the space of sixe howers
and there shall openlie confesse his or her error and offence. And if any person or
persons beinge once conuicted of the same offences as is aforesaide doe eftsoones
perpetrate and comit the like offence. That then euerie such offender beinge of
any the saide offences the second tyme lawfullie and dulie conuicted and
attainted as is aforesaide shall suffer paines of death as a felon or felons,
and shall loose the benefitt and priuiledge of Cleargie and Sanctuarie. And inge
Eniuringe to the Wife of such person as shall offend in any thinge contrarie

James may have had time to pick up something of the continental view of witches in the months he spent in Norway for, when on the return journey they were again subjected to storms, witchcraft of a type rarely seen in England or Scotland was suspected. These suspicions were apparently confirmed by the evidence from the trial of witches of North Berwick in which James took a fascinated interest. Lurid illustrated detail of the North Berwick Trials appeared in a pamphlet called *Newes From Scotland*, which prominently featured grave-robbing and the use of body parts for powder to make the storms. This source may account for the reference to the witches' use of a mutilated corpse in *Macbeth*: 'Here I have a pilot's thumb/Wrecked as homeward he did come'.

The 1604 Act made conjuration using dead bodies a specific offence in England for the first time. It also brought English law

A woodcut of James and 'witches', from *Newes from Scotland*. One shown here is Agnes Sampson, implicated under torture in having caused the storms that had threatened the King and Queen on their voyage back to Scotland, by christening a cat, binding bits of corpses to it and throwing it in the sea while saying 'riddles'. James was disposed to be sceptical, but took threats to the throne very seriously. Agnes Sampson took James to one side and told him the exact words of his conversation with his new wife on their wedding night, a convincing argument of her powers, which ensured her death by burning.

into line with Scottish in making it illegal not only to consult witches for treasonable purposes but also to consult them at all. The evidence of the North Berwick Trials appeared to be tailored to James' liking, for as well as implicating a troublesome political opponent, Francis Hepburn, Earl of Bothwell (the nephew of Mary Queen of Scots' third husband), it included the admission by the Devil, in French, that witchcraft could not harm James because of his godliness.

Though investigations of treasonable witchcraft were likely to provoke widespread interrogation and torture, James tended to approach allegations of witchcraft among his subjects with good sense and humanity. On his royal progress in 1605 he met Richard

A map of Berkshire from 'Theatre of the Empire of Great Britain' by John Norden and John Speede (first published in 1611). Anne Gunter's plight (see document 7) soon attracted the attention of the physicians and divines of Oxford University, and of the King who visited the University on his progress of 1605. James' meeting with Anne at Oxford in August 1605 was followed by two at Finchingbrooke near Windsor in October. Windsor Castle is shown at the top of the map.

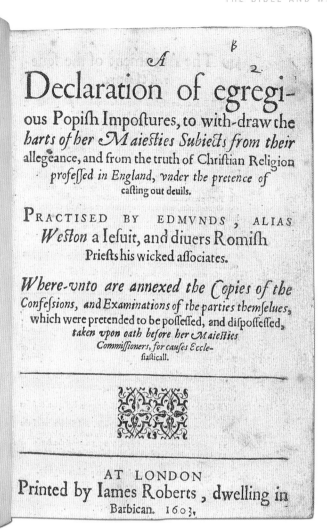

A

Declaration of egregi-

ous Popifh Impoftures, to with-draw the harts of her *Maiefties Subiects from their* allegeance, and from the truth of Chriftian Religion profeffed in England, *vnder the pretence of* cafting out deuils.

Practised by EDMVNDS, ALIAS *Wefton* a Iefuit, and diuers Romifh Priefts his wicked affociates.

Where-vnto are annexed the Copies of the Confefsions, and Examinations of the parties themfelues, which were pretended to be poffeffed, and difpoffeffed, taken vpon oath before her *Maiefties* Commiffioners, for caufes Eccle-fiafticall.

AT LONDON Printed by Iames Roberts, dwelling in Barbican. 1603.

Haydock who claimed to be able to preach in his sleep. James exposed him as a fraud by pretending to be offended by his sleeping sermon and threatening to cut his head off with a sword. The King showed no malice to the impostor and offered to help further his career in the Church, but Haydock preferred the lower profile of a medical career in Salisbury. In this capacity Haydock had examined a still more celebrated victim of bewitchment who came to James' attention soon afterwards.

Anne Gunter appeared to be a victim of witchcraft and exhibited many classic symptoms: vomiting pins, insensibility to pain, foaming at the mouth. In her trances she had named two women from her village who were subsequently acquitted at Berkshire Assizes at Abingdon. If convicted of causing injury through evil spirits the women would have faced the death penalty under the new Act. After the acquittal Anne's father took her to the King at Oxford in October 1605. If he was hoping for a more severe judgement against the supposed witches from James, he was to be disappointed. Instead the result was a Star Chamber case to investigate the validity of the whole business with expert evidence from a whole host of physicians and theologians, including Shakespeare's son-in-law John Hall, and also including Richard Haydock's servant Joan Greene, though there is no statement from the embarrassed Haydock himself.

One of those who questioned Anne Gunter was the Archbishop of Canterbury's chaplain, Samuel Harsnet, who was a famous detector of witchcraft fraud. Harsnet's *Declaration of Egregious Popish Impostures*, published in time to attract the new King's attention, was a major source for the language of demonic possession in Shakespeare's *King Lear*. In the end though, Anne's confession of fraud was coaxed rather than bullied out of her by the prospect of love. Read Anne's evidence in Star Chamber: document 7, *Curing Anne Gunter*.

Title page from *A Declaration of Egregious Popish Impostures* (1603), by Samuel Harsnet, chaplain to Archbishop Bancroft. Harsnet was the man to whom Bancroft entrusted Anne Gunter and whom she feared because of his scepticism. Harsnet's book came in response to a highly successful Catholic missionary campaign to win converts by showing the power of the priest to perform exorcism and the 'Book of Miracles' which reported it.

DOCTOR OF DIVINITY

James' personal interventions did not always have such happy outcomes. The love of religious scholarship, which fuelled his interest in the new Bible, sometimes appeared to be a substitute for policy. He had prepared for the Spanish Armada by penning an extended commentary on the *Book of Revelations*, and celebrated its defeat with his thoughts on five verses of the first book of the *Chronicles*.

James' numerous writings in pamphlets against the Papacy were as much about the political power wielded by the Pope as a maker and deposer of kings, as they were about points of pure theology and they tended to make diplomacy with Catholic countries more difficult afterwards. James carried his scholarship in his head, working from memory rather than referring to his sources, which led to errors and earned him the ridicule of his opponents. One example of this is shown in document 8, *Defender of the faith*. The occasion of this particular pamphlet war was the Oath of Allegiance, which gave Catholics the chance, through outward conformity, to dissociate themselves from those who plotted against the King, most famously in the Gunpowder Plot.

7 *Curing Anne Gunter*

An excerpt from a Star Chamber case, Attorney General v. Gunter 1606. Anne Gunter met the King four times in 1605. Her evidence here is about the potions her father gave her before her meetings with the King, to help her simulate possession. She describes the pressure put on her by her father and by Alice Kirfoote, his ally in the village against the 'witches', to keep the truth about her possession secret from James.

A great many of Brian Gunter's tactics in simulating bewitchment in his daughter came from the witchcraft literature of the time; unfortunately for him it was a literature with which the authorities were also familiar. Samuel Harsnet, Archbishop Bancroft's chaplain, to whom Anne was entrusted, had already detected and published frauds very like Brian Gunter's, using oils and potions to induce symptoms of possession. James' reputation as a witch-hunter had perhaps led Brian Gunter to misjudge the King's likely attitude.

Anne told the King that a potion given to her by a doctor and an amulet about her neck had cured her, but real cure came about through her confession that her possession was simulated and following her removal from the power of her father. Her confession came gradually after her kindly treatment by those to whom James had entrusted her, including Joan Greene the servant of the fraudulent 'sleeping preacher' Richard Haydock. Anne's escape from her father came in the shape of a young man called Asheley, a servant of Bancroft. Asheley seems to have been put up to the job by the authorities, perhaps by the King himself. This may not be the low trick it seems. The power directing Anne Gunter as an unmarried woman was her father who had a vested interest in Anne's bewitchment being believed. Anne's evidence shows that her father explicitly warned her about the dangers of falling under the influence of a young man, perhaps because to take a husband was her only sure way of escaping his power.

ANNE'S EVIDENCE READS:

Previous page

To the sixteenth interrogatory she says that some of the aforesaid green waters were given this deponent at Oxford, some at Windsor and some at Whitehall at such times as his majesty did come to see this deponent. And she says that those waters did first send fumes into her head then make her giddy, then put her into a daze, then lastly cast her into a heavy dullness and into such a sleep as during the same she had no feeling till towards the end of the working of it. And she says that the said waters were given to her by this deponent's said father in the said places last before mentioned. And she further says that when she was to go to Oxford to the King's majesty her said father charged her that she should not forget her oaths of secrecy solemnly by her taken but continue her fits as she was wont [accustomed] to do before. And likewise goodwife Kirfoote did the same day tell her this deponent that if she this deponent did reveal any this which she had sworn to keep secret, the devil would fetch her away both body and soul.

This page, shown

To the seventeenth interrogatory she says that before she was committed to Mr Harsnet she was charged by her said father to take heed that she fell not into love or liking with any man whiles she was [away] from him because that (as he said) might be a means to make her this deponent to depose any secret thing otherwise she intended to have kept them never so close, which she the said Kirfoote's wife did likewise confirm to be true, and therefore she also advised this deponent to take heed of setting her aspect up anew [resuming the appearance of being possessed] as her father had admonished her. After which and some such other speeches her said father spoke to this effect to this deponent viz: Nan: I am sure that all the tortures and punishments that the King can threaten, nor all the fair promises that he can make, can terrify or drive you to confess any thing which you have sworn to keep secret although he should swear to burn you. And the like words this deponent's said father used to her this deponent when she was at Windsor as she says. And further to this interrogatory she cannot depose…

Defender of the faith

Draft proclamation, dated 7 April 1609, recalling James' *An Apologie [Defence] for the Oath of Allegiance*. The proclamation urges everyone who acquired a 'faulty' copy of the tract to exchange it for a 'revised' version. This draft, itself heavily corrected, tries to blame the printer for errors in the original tract, which had prompted widespread ridicule. The errors, though, were mainly of fact rather than of printing.

The revised version of the 'faulty' edition carried James' lengthy 'Premonition to all Christian Princes and Monarchs' which famously identified the Pope as Antichrist. The Christian princes and monarchs who were sent copies either refused them or, if they accepted, did not quite know what to do with them. Henry IV of France called it 'the dullest and most dangerous book ever written on its subject' and reportedly gave it to his court jester.

Possibly the only English monarch who might be called an intellectual, James was fond of debate and especially religious controversy, which he entered into enthusiastically at conferences, at trials and in tracts. But his views on ticklish subjects like the temporal jurisdiction of the Pope tended to make life more difficult for his diplomats. Like so many of James' printed utterances, this piece of work provoked a lively and copious debate among theologians, but made it more difficult than ever for James' Catholic subjects to be loyal to both King and Pope.

THE PROCLAMATION READS:

By the King

Whereas there is lately published in Print our Apologie heretofore made for the Oath of Allegiance, enjoined by Act of Parliament to all our Subjects in certain cases, with a Premonition in our Name dedicated to all Christian Princes and States; which Book by the rashness of the Printer and error of the Examiner, is come forth uncorrected of some faults varying from the Original Copy, and which do not a little pervert the sense: [bracketed text in margin] (Like as we disclaim from all the Copies published before the date hereof, as adulterate, and set out contrary to our express Commandment to the printer given so) our will and pleasure is, and we do hereby straitly [strictly] charge and command all our Subjects, and all others within our Realm, to whose hands any of the said Books be come, that they presently [immediately] and without delay, bring in all such Books as they have, to our Printer; from whom they shall have other Copies for the same, corrected to the truth. And that hereof they fail not, as they will answer to the contrary at their peril.

Second page

Given at our Palace of Westminster, the seventh day of April, in the seventh year of our Reign of Great Britain, France and Ireland.

God save the King

Imprinted at London by Robert Barker, Printer to the King's most Excellent Majesty. In the year 1609

57

Whereas there is lately publish[ed] in print Our
Apologie heretofore made for the oth of Allegiance
enioyned by act of Parlament to all subiects in
certain cases. With a *Premunition* [preface] in Latine dedicated
to all Christian Princes and States which los[t] he
by the expence of the Printer, ~~hour~~ some ven forty
~~~~ ~~~~ accorrupted of some faulte
Like as we defelling arising from the originall dispute and which due
from all the fault
publis[h]ed under ... not with a cittee abert ... the pen... Our will and
pleasure, and present
... respect pleasure therefore is, and we doe hereby, straightly
... againe and astraind will subiectes and all others
within s realme to whose h[an]ds ... of the
s[ai]d book to come that they doe present and
without delay, being in all poynt l[i]ke as the
same is of Printed from whom ther each theme
other copies fr the same corrected b th torty
And that they hereof her fayle not as they will
... at the ... the ther perill

'The Most Horrible Treasons'

PLOTS AND POLITICS

The plot, in 1605, to blow up the King, Lords and Commons in Parliament with gunpowder, the discovery of which is still celebrated on 5 November, seems an almost ordinary occurrence in the context of James' reign in Scotland and early reign in England, so frequent were the plots against him. What made this plot different and why does it remain controversial?

In Scotland James had acquired a well-founded fear of treasonable plots and violent attacks on royal authority, but in his desire to maintain the political balance, which preserved and increased the power of the Crown, he found it difficult to take decisive action against one set of rebellious lords without leaving himself at the mercy of those who remained.

The celebration of Bonfire, Firework or Guy Fawkes Night has lasted nearly 400 years, though it is debatable how many now view it as a celebration of the preservation of the King and Parliament or victory over Catholic rebellion. Perhaps in unleashing fireworks we are siding with the plotters, enacting in miniature the bang that never happened.

It became a familiar tradition in Scottish plots against him, to kidnap the King and put a sword to his throat as a negotiating position from which the plotters would somehow emerge with high office and a lasting influence on policy. Vulnerable though James was, especially during his minority, he had a happy knack of turning such plots to his political advantage, so that some people came to suspect that he had engineered the events or conspired in them.

The Scottish plot that James was most keen his English subjects should remember was the Gowrie Conspiracy of 5 August 1600. The official version of events was clearly incredible: mysterious strangers, crocks of gold, familiar spirits, and the King's own unearthly powers of rhetoric in successfully pleading for his life. Central as usual was the desire of the plotters to persuade the King of their reasonable demands, with the added insurance of threatened imprisonment and assassination. The conspiracy was also convenient in its outcome, provoking a skirmish which eliminated some powerful political opponents, and was good for James' popularity, being commemorated in public holidays and sermons of thanksgiving.

In England there were plots of similar character against James even before the Gunpowder Plot. Given that James' succession was largely unopposed, the number of plots against him might seem odd, but they were generally aimed at forcing a change in policy or a change of councillors. Even those which aimed to replace him, apart from some wild designs to crown the Infanta of Spain, planned to supplant him with members of his own dynasty. Two plots were uncovered soon after James' accession: the Bye or Secondary Plot which aimed to present a petition of Catholic grievances and then enforce it, and the Main Plot, which added the threat of assistance from Spanish forces in Flanders.

Both the Main and Bye Plots were abortive but had the celebrated effect of implicating Sir Walter Raleigh in treason. Raleigh had become a focus of discontent after James' accession, losing his position as Captain of the Guard to a Scot and having to give Durham House back to the Bishop of Durham. Historians have understandably doubted whether England's great champion of sea power against Spain was really involved in a Spanish-backed plot to depose the King of England. It is possible, though, that Raleigh planned to regain credit by delivering the plotters himself to the King, but that the conspirators were exposed by others before he got the chance.

In fact the combination of Catholics and Protestants in these plots was not as incredible as it might seem. The focus of the discontent was the possibility of a treaty with Spain, which became a reality in 1604. Essex's rebellion had ostensibly favoured an anti-Spanish policy and feared Cecil's pro-Spanish intentions but had attracted Catholic support because a Spanish treaty ended hopes of help from abroad, which might install a Catholic government. The Catholic plots of 1603 had attracted Protestant support because with James being guided by Cecil, a Spanish treaty was inevitable. How these groups would have co-operated had the rebellions and conspiracies been successful is difficult to imagine.

BACKGROUND TO THE GUNPOWDER PLOT

Gunpowder plotters Robert Catesby, Thomas Winter and John and Christopher Wright had all been involved in Essex's rebellion. The motivation of the plot has often been cited as disappointed Catholic hopes of James' religious policy, but in truth these men had been plotting well before they had a chance to be disappointed. The true spur to their actions was not just James' indifference but also their abandonment by Spain.

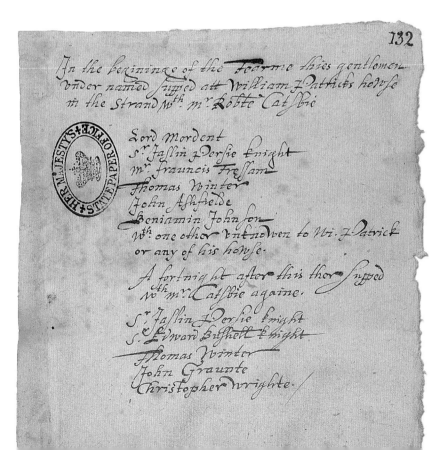

A list of Gunpowder Plot suspects. The heading reads 'In the beginning of the term [Michaelmas 1605] the gentlemen under named supped at William Patrick's house in the Strand with Mr Robert Catesby'. Among them is Francis Tresham, the probable author of the Monteagle letter, and Ben Jonson who offered his services to Cecil when the plot was discovered. Were either or both spying on the plotters in October?

This element has lent the plot some of its romance as the affair was based on a quixotic hope of backing from Spain, which the conspirators could not really have expected. Then there was a desperate determination to press on alone when this, as well as support from the English Catholic gentry and other Englishmen who were generally against their foreign ruler, in turn failed to materialize. Guy Fawkes' most consistent ideological line in his confessions was simple xenophobia rather than religious conviction, a desire to blow James and his Scottish governors 'back to Scotland'.

THE PLAN

Initially the plotters were fortunate. They had first planned to lay a mine; Fawkes, who had fought for the Spanish forces against the Dutch, seems to have been recruited for this purpose. While tunnelling beneath the parliament building they heard a rushing noise above them, which turned out to be not the roof of the tunnel falling in, but the coal merchant in the vault above clearing out. They acquired the vault for themselves, resolving to fill it with gunpowder and gratefully gave up mining. Then things began to go wrong; commissioners for the Union commandeered their

The Gunpowder Plot conspirators (engraving, 1606). The conspirators are shown whispering and passing secret notes, but socially at their ease. This conspiracy of gentlemen was unusual in seeming to lack either popular support or aristocratic sponsorship, despite the attempts of James' government to discover both.

Robert Winter Christopher wright John wright Thomas Percy Guido Fawkes Robert Catesby Thomas Winto Bates

The delivery of the Monteagle letter, from *Mischeefes Mysterie: or Treasons Master-peece, the Powder-plot*, by John Vickers (woodcut, 1617). James was hunting, rather than sitting in state, when the letter betraying the plot came into the government's hands, and the reaction to it was rather more chaotic than it appears here. Nonetheless the speed and success of Cecil's investigation of the plot was sufficient to imply government complicity. The Monteagle letter itself replaced 'you' with 'some of your friends' in its opening line as if to distance Monteagle himself from the plotters.

Westminster lodgings for their deliberations, the opening of Parliament was delayed by plague, and then they learned of a letter betraying the plot.

Against a background of a multitude of unlikely plots, James' Council had to take warning and threatening letters seriously, but it was more difficult to know how much credibility to attach to them. Cecil's reaction to the letter passed to the Council by Lord Monteagle seems to have been sceptical. In the official account of events, James, in his Old Testament wisdom as a Joseph or a Daniel, returned from his hunting at Royston on 31 October, was shown the letter and immediately grasped its significance to the admiration of his hitherto mystified councillors. This is not quite as incredible as it sounds; James' father had been killed in a gunpowder explosion, and James was always sensitive to the possibilities of assassination. Monteagle himself had been associated with Essex's rebels and Jesuit priests and needed to cultivate credit with the authorities, not least because he was an old friend of Thomas Percy. Read the Monteagle letter: document 9, *'A terrible blow'*.

9 'A terrible blow'

An anonymous letter given to Lord Monteagle, 26 October 1605. This letter, giving a thinly veiled warning of the Gunpowder Plot, has aroused as much speculation as any other letter in British history. The questions of who wrote it and to what extent James' government manufactured and controlled the plot have prompted widespread, even wild speculation.

On 26 October 1605 Monteagle returned to his house at Hoxton for the first time in several weeks. That same day, a 'reasonable tall' stranger, his features fortuitously concealed by the twilight, left a letter with a servant of the house who happened to be outside; this was passed to another servant who Monteagle asked to read it aloud while he ate. This has been taken as evidence both of Monteagle's innocence and his complicity in the plot.

The plotters themselves identified the author of the warning letter as Monteagle's brother-in-law Francis Tresham, a lukewarm plotter who had offered Catesby money to forget the whole thing. Among those ingeniously supposed to have written the letter was Cecil himself, keen to show off the efficiency of his intelligence network by inventing a plot for it to uncover. The heavily disguised and archly illiterate letter certainly suggests a writer known to Monteagle, who wished to conceal his identity, though it has been suggested that Thomas Phelippes, Francis Walsingham's chief decipherer and the annotator of the 'Gallows Letter' which helped send James' mother, Mary Queen of Scots to her death, might have been the man who concocted it.

Francis Tresham died suddenly in the Tower and was buried with great haste, a sure sign to the conspirators that he had been poisoned to stop him talking and that the authorities were keen to dispose of the evidence. Other sources suggest he died of a disease which made quick burial advisable.

THE LETTER READS:

My lord, out of the love I bear to some of your friends, I have a care of your preservation, therefore I would advise you as you tender your life to devise some excuse to shift your attendance at this parliament, for God and man have concurred to punish the wickedness of this time, and think not slightly of this advertisement, but retire yourself into your country, where you may expect the event in safety, for though there be no appearance of any stir, yet I say they shall receive a terrible blow this parliament and yet they shall not see who hurts them, this counsel is not to be condemned because it may do you good and can do you no harm, for the danger is past as soon as you have burnt the letter and I hope God will give you the grace to make good use of it, to whose holy protection I commend you.

my lord out of the love i beare to some of youere frends i
have a caer of youer preservacion therfor i would
advyse yowe as yowe tender youer lyf to devyse some
excuse to shift of youer attendance at this parleament
for god and man hathe concurred to punishe the wickednes
of this tyme and thinke not slightlye of this advertisment
but retyere youre self into youer contri wheare yowe
maye expect the event in safti for thowghe theare be no
apparance of anni stir yet i saye they shall receyve a terrible
blowe this parleament and yet they shall not seie who
hurts them this councel is not to be contemned becauso
it maye do yowe good and can do yowe no harme for the
dangere is passed as soon as yowe have burnt the letter
and i hope god will give yowe the grace to mak good
use of it to whose holy protecion i comend yowe

Thomas Percy had friends and official business in Westminster, so it was he who had acquired the vault and lodgings there. Percy was a 'gentleman pensioner', a member of the King's Bodyguard, an appointment he had received from his cousin Henry Percy, Earl of Northumberland. From this position it was his job to execute the next part of the plot after Parliament and the King had been blown up; this was to kidnap the next heir and ensure, after an appropriate Catholic education, he or she was put at the head of a Catholic government. There was considerable doubt about the detail of this part of the plot. First, it was not at all clear who the next heir would be. Prince Henry might attend Parliament himself and be a victim of the explosion, and even at the age of 11 he was an unlikely candidate for conversion to Catholicism. Therefore, Charles or Elizabeth were considered more promising. Second, the plotters did not know or would not say who would head the Catholic protectorate.

To allow the plot to ripen, nothing further was done until 4 November. James hoped that, as the plan progressed, not merely those who were involved in its mechanics, but also those in power who were supporting them would be revealed. An initial tour by the Earl of Suffolk – as Lord Chamberlain he was responsible for preparations for the new Parliament – accompanied by Monteagle, provided the authorities with all the evidence they could have hoped for. They found Fawkes overseeing a large quantity of firewood in a vault rented by his master Thomas Percy. Monteagle made a few pointed remarks to Suffolk as they returned, about being previously unaware of Percy, a Catholic, renting a cellar in Westminster. Fawkes was arrested and the gunpowder discovered, but Percy's position and connections made him the key to understanding who the real power was behind the plot and the identity of the head of the planned Catholic protectorate. On 5 November 1605 a proclamation was drafted for Thomas Percy's arrest: document 10, *A traitor with a 'good face'*.

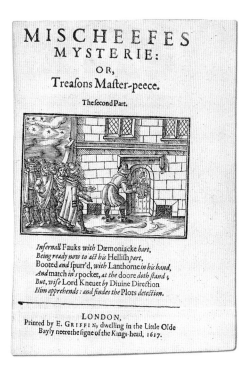

Title page to *Mischeefes Mysterie: or Treasons Master-peece*. This poem of 1617 celebrates James' prophetic powers in deciphering the Monteagle letter and does it in iambic pentameter: 'And though this Letter seems most obscure, Like great Apollo's Delphean Mystery, Yet I a Joseph, Daniel will procure, T'untwine the twist of its obscurity'. The poem also includes an epigram attacking the Jesuits; the plot of a few desperate gentlemen has become an international Catholic conspiracy.

ROUNDING UP THE CONSPIRATORS

At this stage all the authorities had to go on was Fawkes and his connection with Percy. In their quest for information about the whereabouts of the plotters, the authorities turned to Simon Forman, astrologer and physician, a move that to modern eyes appears rather bizarre. Though finding out the location of lost and sought after people and objects was a standard part of Forman's trade, it is probable that his knowledge of the lives of his patients rather than his powers of divination were the real reason why Forman was consulted. He was known to have Catholic connections; the patients who consulted him most frequently and confidentially were the wives of London Catholics, who came to him, if we are to believe his diary, for his particular and unethical brand of fertility treatment.

10

A traitor with a 'good face'

Proclamation for the apprehension of Thomas Percy, dated 5 November 1605. This hastily drafted proclamation orders the discovery and arrest of the man who had rented the cellar beneath the Houses of Parliament in which the gunpowder was found.

The detailed, rather complimentary description of Thomas Percy reveals that he was well known in court circles. At this stage the conspiracy looks like an inside job, the personal betrayal of a few individuals in positions of trust. Even Fawkes himself had been to a wedding attended by the King earlier in the year, a fact omitted from his published confession. As the investigation widened and more suspects were drawn in, the personal element was submerged and the usual hard core of malcontents was

blamed. Since many of the plotters had been involved in the Essex rebellion against Elizabeth I, this was a reasonable view to take, but rather ironic given the positive overtures James had made to the Essex party at that time.

The Percy connection made the obvious candidate for the real power behind the plot Henry Percy, 9th Earl of Northumberland, the head of one of England's most powerful Catholic families. Ostensibly, it was unlikely that the Earl would betray James since the King had rehabilitated him, like so many others, after political isolation under Elizabeth. The 7th Earl had been executed after the Northern Rebellion in 1572, and the 8th shot himself while imprisoned on suspicion of complicity in plots to free James' mother, Mary Queen of Scots, from

prison. Thomas Percy, a cousin of the Earl, was a collector of his rents and constable of his castle at Alnwick. Crucially, as it became clear, it was the Earl who had failed to administer the Oath of Supremacy, which would have precluded Percy, as a practising Catholic, from being a member of James' bodyguard or 'gentleman pensioner'. Increasingly the authorities attempted to implicate the Earl in the plot. He was held prisoner on suspicion of complicity for 16 years but then released in an amnesty.

Despite the urging of the proclamation to 'keep him alive' Thomas Percy was killed in the siege at Holbeach, prompting further speculation that he might otherwise have implicated the Earl or Cecil or whomever else you believe was behind the Gunpowder Plot.

THE PROCLAMATION READS:

Whereas one Thomas Percy, a Gentleman Pensioner to his Majesty, is discovered to have been privy to [aware of] one of the most horrible Treasons that ever was contrived, that is, to have blown up this day, while his Majesty should have been in the upper House of the Parliament, attended with the Queen, the Prince, all his nobility and the Commons, with Gunpowder [bracketed text in margin] (for which purpose a great quantity of Powder was conveyed into a Vault under the said Chamber, which is this morning there found) the Chamber where they should be assembled, which Percy is sithens [afterwards] fled:

These are to will and command all our Officers and loving Subjects whatsoever, to do that which we doubt not but they will

willingly perform, according to the former experience We have had of their love and zeal towards [us], That is, to make all diligent search for the said Percy, and to apprehend him by all possible means, especially to keep him alive, to the end the rest of the Conspirators may be discovered. The said Percy is a tall man, with a great broad beard, a good face, the colour of his beard and head mingled with white hairs, but the head more white than the beard, he stoops somewhat in the shoulders, well coloured in the face, long footed, small [thin] legged.

Given at our Palace of Westminster, the fifth day of November, 1605, in the third year of our reign of Great Britain.

of Novembr 1605

The government's view was that the plotters came from a group of disaffected men who simply used the cloak of religion to justify their actions. Despite this, their eventual success in implicating Jesuit priests in the plot has been seen as part of an attempt to turn the plot investigation into an anti-Catholic witch-hunt. In fact James had consistently distinguished between ordinary Catholics and the Jesuits, whom he saw as the political agents of the Papacy as a maker and destroyer of kings. In a sense, the government wanted to show how these troublemakers turned Catholics into rebels.

James was fascinated by the plotters and their motives and had to be dissuaded by his councillors from his desire to interview them personally. On the day after the proclamation against Thomas Percy, James framed the questions to be used in the interrogation of 'John Johnson' whose real identity was not yet known (see document 11, *Torturing Guy Fawkes*). James linked him to the malcontents who opposed the creation of 'Great Britain' and was prepared to use all the powers at his disposal to discover any links with the Catholic missionary priesthood.

The conspirators next attempted to raise a rebellion in the Midlands but support did not materialize from the Catholic gentry or from the people generally. They made a last stand at Holbeach on 8 November when, in an ironic twist of events, their store of gunpowder, intended for the rebellion, blew up accidentally. The authorities would have preferred the plotters to have been taken alive, but Catesby and Percy fighting back to back were killed by a single shot and with them went the chance of truly establishing the connection with the Earl of Northumberland.

The number of suspects increased and still more plots were uncovered, even an earlier scheme against Queen Elizabeth involving a number of the Gunpowder Plotters, allied with Spain. An account of this 'Spanish Treason' was omitted from the official account of the Gunpowder Plot for reasons of diplomacy. Strenuous attempts were made to implicate Raleigh in this plot too.

Rumour, debate and scepticism about the Gunpowder Plot began early. Dudley Carleton, the diplomat and letter-writer, heard reports in Paris as early as 13 November 1605 that 'there was no such matter, nor anything near it more than a barrel of powder found near the Court'. Carleton found himself in a minor and temporary disgrace having been among those who helped Percy find lodging in Westminster.

Suspicion in the country that Cecil had engineered the whole thing was first recorded as early as December 1605, partly because, in the face of rumour and gradually emerging information, the investigative operation moved so quickly and successfully. Ultimately, though the Gunpowder Plot was never 'solved', and this is part of the appeal when compared to an earlier plot like the Gowrie Conspiracy, there are few loose ends and few grounds for conspiracy theory.

James enforced the Oath of Allegiance in the aftermath of the plot, intending to give Catholics a chance to make a profession of loyalty to the Crown and dissociate themselves from the plotters. In a sense the failed Midlands rising had proved that Catholic support for rebellion was tepid, but the Oath came to be seen as branding all Catholics as rebels or potential rebels and to this extent the plot marked another significant stage in the formal separation of Catholics from the heart of English society.

The 'dark' lantern Guy Fawkes is said to have been carrying on his arrest. It has a hinged door which was once fitted with a window made of horn through which the light would glow. The vent at the top would have let out the heat. This vent is attached to an inner cylinder which could be rotated in order to conceal the light, and Fawkes himself.

11

Torturing Guy Fawkes

An undated letter, though probably of 6 November 1605, from James to the Council, regarding the questioning of Guy Fawkes. Written in his own hand, James himself framed the questions that should be asked and here details the tortures to be used on Guy Fawkes. The two-page letter links the plotters to those who opposed the creation of 'Great Britain'.

Once accused of high treason the chances of acquittal were very slight. So grave was the charge that evidence inadmissible in a modern court, rumour, evidence obtained under torture and the paid evidence of informers, was amassed and credited. Ben Jonson appears in State Papers at this point, not as the regime's courtly entertainer of the masque or the satirist of the public stages, but in a shadowy letter to Cecil apparently offering his services as an informer on the Catholic circles in which he moved freely.

All the details of Fawkes' life were given falsely to begin with. His war wound from fighting for Spain in the Netherlands was explained as a scar of pleurisy. For a time Fawkes was the only member in government hands of a rebellion reportedly spreading across the Midlands; in the official questioning the mixture of care and brutality in dealing with him reflects the urgency of the situation and the ignorance of the authorities of the real motives and sponsors of the plot. Comparison of Fawkes' signatures (see below) on his first and second confessions provides evidence that tortures, whether of the gentler variety or the less gentle, were used.

JAMES WROTE:

First page

The examinate would now be made to answer to formal interrogators:

1. As what he is (for I can never yet hear of any man that knows him)?
2. Where was he born?
3. What were his parents' names?
4. What age is he of?
5. Where has he lived?
6. How he has lived and by what trade of life?
7. How he received those wounds on his breast?
8. If he was ever in service with any other before Percy, and what they were, and how long?
9. How came he in Percy's service, by what means and at what time?
10. What time was this house hired by his master?
11. And how soon after the possessing of it did he begin his devilish preparations?
12. When and where learned he to speak French?
13. What gentlewoman's letter it was that was found upon him?
14. And wherefore [why] does she give him another name in it than he gives to himself?
15. If he was ever a papist, and if so who brought him up in it?
16. If otherwise, how was he converted, where, when, and by whom?

The course of his life I am the more desirous to know because I have divers [various] motives leading me to suspect that he has remained long beyond the seas and either is a priest or has long served some priest or fugitive abroad, for I can yet (as I said in beginning hereof) meet with no man that knows him. The letter found upon him gives him another name, and those that best know his master can never remember to have seen him in his company,

Second page, shown

whereupon it should seem that he has been recommended by persons to his master's service only for this use, wherein only he has served him. And therefore he would also be asked in what company and ship he went out of England, and the port he shipped at, and the same questions would be asked anent [about] the form of his return. As for these trumpery wares [superstitious objects, perhaps a crucifix or rosary] found on him, the signification and use of every one of them would be known. And what I have observed in them the bearer will show you. Now last, you remember of the cruelly villainous pasquil [satire] that railed upon me for the name of Britain. If I remember right, it spoke something of harvest and prophesied my destruction about that time. You may think of this for it is like to be the labour of such a desperate fellow as this is.

If he will not otherwise confess, the gentler tortures are to be first used on him, *et sic per gradus ad ima tenditur* [and so by degrees until the ultimate is reached], and so God speed your good work.

James R.

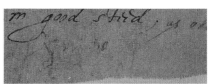

quhair upon it shoulde seeme that he hadi bene ~~reccomendit~~ reccomendit by
some personnis to his maisters service only for this use, quhairin only he
hath servid him, & thairfore he wolde ~~not~~ also be asked in quhat company & ship
he went out of englande, & the porte he shipped at, & the lyke quaestions
wolde be ~~not~~ asked anent the forme of his returne, as for these trompet
warres founde upon him, the signifacation & ~~used~~ use of everie one of
thaime wolde be knowin, & quhat I have observid in thaim, the bearare
will shore you, now taste ye remember of the crewallie villanouse pasquil
that rayled upon me for the name of brittaine, if I remember ride
it spake some thing of harvest & prophecied my destruction about that
tyme, ye maye thinke of this, for it is lyke to be the laboure of suche a
desperate fellow as this is, if he will not other wayes confesse, the gentle
tortours are to be first usid unto him, & sic per gradus ad ima tendituur,
& so god speide youre gode worke.

                                                James R

The British Solomon

KING, COUNCIL AND JUSTICE

James had a personal interest in justice, which earned him the title 'The British Solomon' among his subjects as well as flattering courtiers. At the same time James' court has been accused of corrupting justice through personal favouritism and greed. The Milward and Overbury cases, celebrated in the literature of the period, illustrate both elements and the extent of royal power.

James not only governed through his Privy Council but also dispensed justice through it. The Council sat, usually twice a week, in a judicial capacity as the Court of Star Chamber. To us Star Chamber has an evil reputation for handing out vindictive punishments without regard for the law of the land, a reputation largely earned after James' death, by Charles I, who used the court as a weapon against his political opponents. To many contemporaries, however, Star Chamber was a welcome direct recourse to royal justice in cases where the ordinary course of law had failed or been corrupted by locally powerful individuals. To James it was a tool of royal authority and a source of revenue, but it was also a forum which allowed him to indulge his scholarly passions.

THE MILWARD CASE

The first year of James' reign saw a record number of Star Chamber cases. One in particular aroused James' personal interest because the man at the centre of the case was a Doctor of Divinity, John Milward, whom James had earmarked for clerical preferment. The case tells the story of Agnes Howe who inherited her aunt's fortune at 17, and was promptly betrothed by her father to several suitors

Illuminated initial from the Court of King's Bench: *Coram Rege* Roll (Easter Term, 1623). This stylized image of the monarch shows James as the symbol of justice, dressed in regalia which changed little from reign to reign, but the buckled shoes and the cut of the King's beard are recognizably Jacobean.

and subjected to a variety of ecclesiastical court judgements about the validity of her 'marriages'. John Milward had married Agnes in 1601 but after a questionable judgement in the ecclesiastical appeal court in February 1603, apparently influenced by a play by George Chapman, he was ordered to give her up to a man with a prior contract. The case, which amounts to 250 pages of paper and parchment, makes it pretty clear that whatever the faults of James' court it did not invent corruption in matrimonial cases or pure greed, which were both

St Paul's Cross. John Milward preached here in April 1605 only months after his marriage to Agnes Howe was finally declared legal, while the scandal was still fresh in the minds of his hearers. This occasion was reported by John Chamberlain, as providing an ironic commentary on the preacher: 'Dr. Milwood preaching at Paul's Cross in the middest of the sermon, a cuckoo came flying over the pulpit (a thing I never saw nor heard of before) and very lewdly called and cried out with open mouth'.

thriving during Elizabeth's reign. Read about the case, and see the evidence of one deponent in document 12, *Rescuing a royal chaplain*.

Milward was duly made a royal chaplain and died loyally in 1609 engaged in the failed Jacobean project to convert the Scottish Kirk to the virtues of Anglican Church government. In 1610 his brother, who also found a wife among the deponents in the case, published the sermon that John Milward had preached in 1607 in thanksgiving for James' deliverance from the Gowrie Conspiracy of 1600. *On Jacob's Great day of Trouble and Deliverance* appeared with an Epistle Dedicatory, which boasts that James 'did out of his heroic and princely clemency, a compassionate pitier of wronged simplicity, rescue him [John Milward] from the jaws of conspiring perjury'.

On Milward's part there was perhaps more than just a desire to flatter the King by giving thanks for James' deliverance from the Gowrie Conspiracy seven years after the event. Perhaps Milward felt that the conspiracy against him in the matter of his marriage to Agnes had begun then too and he was giving thanks for his own deliverance.

THE OVERBURY CASE

If the Milward case presented avarice across a broad social spectrum in London the Overbury case was a still more potent mix of murder, power, sex and royal favouritism. For many it is the ultimate expression of the poisonous moral atmosphere of James' court. The most prominent masque of 1606 celebrated the marriage of Frances Howard to the Earl of Essex. James sought to unite couples as well as kingdoms and this was an attempt to finally cement the re-alliance he had begun in broadening his Privy Council by bringing together the Catholic Howard faction and the son of the rebellious Earl of Essex. Rather like the union of England and Scotland the marriage failed despite royal approval, a failure complicated by the fact that Frances Howard's lover was the chief royal favourite, Robert Carr.

Robert Carr had come south with the King in 1603 but only came to James' attention after a fall from his horse in 1607. James had not placed Scots in the highest offices in England but he chose advisers from his Scottish entourage to act in his personal

Portrait of Sir Thomas Overbury. His death, largely unmourned at the time, became the scandal of the age when the great favourite and the King himself were implicated. Sir Edward Coke conducted a far-reaching enquiry, which earned him James' displeasure for uncovering plots to kill Prince Henry with magic; perhaps the King feared he too would be implicated in these. The investigation was handed to Francis Bacon instead. For once Coke failed to implicate Sir Walter Raleigh because of, or perhaps despite, the fact that he was already in the Tower.

Rescuing a royal chaplain

Star Chamber case, Attorney General v. Joanes, Howe, Flasket, Field, Oswald, Daniell, Shawe, Chapman, Pearce, Woodford, 1603. This case centred on John Milward, one of the King's witty, worldly clerics, who was soon to be made a royal chaplain. The case hinged on whether or not Milward's bride of 1601, Agnes Howe, had already been contracted to another man in August 1600 and whether a court decision against Milward in February 1603 had been influenced by perjured witnesses or a notorious stage play on the subject. The 'other husband' was John Flasket, a bookbinder and bookseller trading in St Paul's churchyard in London, and the case had been the source of scandalous gossip in that centre of scandalous gossip for three years. The play, now sadly lost, was George Chapman's *The Old Joiner of Aldgate*, performed by the company of child actors in St Paul's itself. Some of the parties in the case had the dubious pleasure of seeing themselves impersonated on stage under assumed but transparent names.

The key witness in the case was Rose Oswald who had wanted the match between Agnes and Flasket, and had believed a verbal contract, sufficient in Canon Law, had passed between them, but had not herself heard it. Under pressure from her husband and from Flasket she deposed that she had heard it, and was too scared of her husband to confess her lie. The extract transcribed here suggests, perhaps flatteringly, that Rose's confession finally came on hearing of James' interest in the case. She felt she would be physically incapable of lying to the King.

Agnes Blundell who recounts Rose Oswald's agonies of conscience here was not a wholly reliable witness herself. Witnesses for Flasket also alleged she had beaten her husband, been judicially whipped and thrown into Bridewell prison. Milward seems to have been an accomplished manipulator, hiring a servant, Edmund Brampton, apparently for the purpose of following and suborning witnesses. 'One that was by', whose identity Agnes Blundell carefully conceals in her evidence, was almost certainly Milward or Brampton who were alleged to have offered Rose financial inducements and freedom from prosecution for perjury if she changed her evidence.

AGNES BLUNDELL'S EVIDENCE READS:

[beginning of deposition] Agnes the wife of Edward Blundell of St. Mary Magdalen, London, Stationer aged 42 years or thereabouts f.187 26 June 1603...

...And further this deponent says that the said Rose Oswald out of the grief of her heart did on Sunday last was fortnight [a fortnight ago last Sunday] say unto her this deponent that she was afraid the cause would now come before the King and then she should never be able to stand in it [stick to her story] but she must needs speak the truth and 'were I not better now', said she the said Rose, 'to reveal it, than to be brought before the King, for I take God to witness, said she, I never heard nor saw any such thing and then I must needs declare it, and speak the truth. And the said Rose Oswald then also said to this deponent if I could tell how to get the truth revealed and might come to no hurt, I would fain [gladly] reveal it. It is well done, said one that was by, to ease your conscience and clear it...

So that her husband came hast[e]
and she that she was throwne alwaye
at [Wor]churche So y[a]t her [husba]n[d]
She w[oul]d booth throwne to g[r]ise and
fell & [th]e depon[en]t sayth that [th]e
sd [th]e [Ri]chall dyd of[t]e hyr[s]
[of] her harte dyd [a fi]t m[y]ss
on Sunday[e] [nex]t was [fort]nigh[t] say[e]
but s[h]e [th]e [the] depon[en]t that [s]he was
afrayd[e] w[h]en y[e] rav[i]e woul[d] come
[wh]ere she b[ein]g cruelly s[h]e coul[d]
be n[ever] able to stande in it but s[he]
m[u]st need[e]s [ov]ertake [s]he [tim]e[s] and w[ere]
[I] no[t] better no[w] said [s]he [s]e [hel]p[ed] [th]y[ne]
to reveale it [th]e[m] to be broughte before
[th]e king for I tak[e] god to w[itn]es said
[s]he [I] [n]eu[er] hard nor saw any such
[th]ing and t[h]en I my[s]t need[e]s declare
it and [sp]eake [s]he truth and [th]e[y]
[th]yne [Ri]chall [th]en allg[e] [s]ayd to [th]y[n]
[Iep] i[f] I wo[u]ld tell [s]o[m]e to tell [th]e
truth to reveal [i]t m[yght] come to no hurt
I would fayne reveale y[t]. Th[i]s
[we]ll done[n] sayd one [th]at was by
to day [th]e [m]u[r]der [i]s [r]eveal[e] [Mr] [W]her[ri]
[h]elpd [th]y[ne] was ad[v]ysd by [th]e[m] [th]e

interest and, in James' view, in the broader interests of his kingdoms, rather than in the narrow and vested interests of the English
State and of his English advisers themselves. In Carr he saw some-
one with no power base or financial interests, who would be
dependent on the King and act for him alone. Carr invited James'
confidence, appeared grave and devoted, and was undoubtedly
attractive to James, who nursed him after his accident. Carr grew in
influence. The stream of suitors, which had beset James' progress
south, had never really abated and James had grown weary of
them. Carr began sifting suits, seeking out the King's advantage
and becoming the means of access to him.

Carr became Viscount Rochester in 1611 and by then had begun
his courtship of Frances Howard. In this he had the help of the
letters and verses of Thomas Overbury. Overbury was involved
in the factional politics which James had sought to suppress, and
he attempted to win favour with Carr and draw him into the
anti-Spanish party. Now his
efforts threatened to promote
alliance between Carr and the
leading pro-Spanish faction
represented by the Howard
family, and his relationship
with Carr changed. Nevertheless, Overbury boasted of his
influence with Carr and, by
extension, with the King.

Frances Howard drugged her
husband and sought divorce
on the grounds of non-con-
summation, which did not

Robert Carr and Frances
Howard, the Earl and
Countess of Somerset.
Jealous of the friends of
his favourites, James was
nonetheless genuinely
concerned that they
should marry and to their
advantage. He supported
Frances Howard's divorce
from the Earl of Essex and
her marriage to Robert
Carr against opposition
from lawyers and church-
men. John Donne profited
from the fall of Overbury,
replacing him as Carr's
secretary. He offered to
write a reasoned defence
of his patron's marriage
but was persuaded to write
a celebratory marriage
poem instead.

The portraiture of Robert Car Earle of Somerset Vicount Rochester, Knight of the most
noble order of the Garter &c. And of the Ladie Francis his wife.

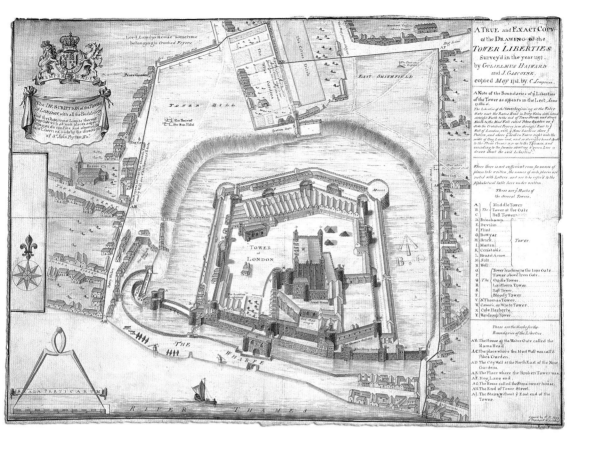

'A True and Exact Copy of the Draught of the Tower Liberties surveyed in the year 1597 by Gulielmus Haiward and J. Gascoyne.' Though it was a place of execution, torture and imprisonment, the Tower of London was also an ancient royal residence which could house its aristocratic and wealthy prisoners in some style with their books and servants. Henry Percy, Earl of Northumberland continued his chemical experiments, and Sir Walter Raleigh composed feverishly in verse and prose.

draw a confession from the Earl, even though he might have been glad to be rid of her. She then changed tack suggesting he was not naturally impotent, but bewitched into impotence with her alone. Carr was afraid Overbury would discredit him while the divorce proceedings were going through. In this spirit James offered Overbury a posting overseas which was diplomatic in two senses. When Overbury justifiably but dangerously refused the appointment James was furious and sent him to the Tower. Carr tried to give the impression he was working for his friend's release, but he was secretly glad to have him out of the way.

James appointed commissioners to examine the validity of the Essex marriage he had engineered and celebrated, and to consider the possibility of divorce. Like the Milward case, it presented James with an appealing opportunity to forward the interest of a favourite and indulge his unhealthy interest in their sexual relations. The commission, composed of judges and senior churchmen, generally opposed the divorce of the unhappy couple until James pressured them individually. Their vote was still split even after all his efforts so James appointed two more commissioners who favoured the divorce, which was granted on 25 September 1613.

In the midst of the commissioners' deliberations on 15 September 1613, Thomas Overbury died in the Tower. He had taken an awful lot of killing. Frances Howard had tried to poison Overbury through his keeper Richard Weston, who was appointed for the purpose, but was prevented by Sir Gervase Helwys, the Lieutenant of the Tower – although he dared not name Frances Howard as the poisoner because she was too powerful. She eventually succeeded in killing Overbury by bribing an apothecary's boy to administer a poisoned enema.

Frances Howard and Carr were married on 26 December 1613 amid lavish festivities and masques. Carr was created Earl of Somerset so that Frances Howard could remain a countess. Only in 1615 did Helwys confess his strong suspicions about Overbury's death, but by that time a new favourite was rising to eclipse Carr: the star of the twelfth night masque of 1615, George Villiers.

Overbury's death implicated the King because by ordering his imprisonment James had made the murder possible. James was desperate that justice should appear to be done in the case, but that did not stop him interfering. Read the King's letter to the commissioners: document 13, *Losing a favourite*.

The couple were found guilty and faced the death penalty, but James' keenness for justice being seen to be done did not extend to the sentence being carried out on his favourite. Fittingly enough the Earl and Countess were imprisoned in the Tower until 1622 when they were released to acrimonious country obscurity.

PLAYS, PROSE AND KINGLY POWER

Lawrence Lisle, the publisher of the latest news on the Overbury scandal, had been apprenticed to John Flasket, the 'other husband' of Agnes Howe in the Milward case. Lisle had deposed twice in the case and would certainly have been impressed with the financial success that the scandal brought to Chapman's play. In defence of the play its promoter pointed out in his Star Chamber evidence that it had been performed in a 'private' theatre. It had been staged in the precincts of St Paul's Cathedral by its company of child actors (who had traditionally given court performances and who performed at James' coronation progress through London) and had been licensed by the Master of the Revels. In a sense he was representing the play as a masque, a private entertainment authorized by the King. In fact the play had been altered to make the parallels with real events more obvious after it had been licensed and in reality there was no real distinction between the popular impact of this 'private' theatre and the public stages like the Globe. The explosion of books and pamphlets about the Overbury case, Lawrence Lisle's publications among them, were likewise apparently under royal control, licensed by the Stationers' Company and regulated through Star Chamber. In the later years of James' reign this gap between the apparent powers of the King and his ability to exert control widened.

The modern reconstruction of the Globe theatre near the site of the original Globe at Bankside. The Globe was summer home of The King's Men who wintered indoors at Blackfriars. Seats at the Globe were cheaper than at the 'private' theatre at St Paul's but comparable if you added the price of the ferry. The Globe was one of two public theatres in London licensed at the beginning of the reign; by the end there were seven despite the best efforts of the city authorities to close them down.

13 *Losing a favourite*

James' directions for the commissioners in the Overbury case, October 1615. After the confession of the Lieutenant of the Tower, Sir Gervase Helwys, of his knowledge of the attempts on Sir Thomas Overbury's life, trials and executions followed in a blaze of scandalous publicity. Helwys detailed the numerous poisoning attempts on Overbury, not merely the vial of poison, which he intercepted, but pies and jellies filled with poison given to him through his keeper Richard Weston.

These directions were sent to the commissioners in the interval between Weston's first arraignment on 19 October 1615 when, under pressure from allies of the Earl and Countess of Somerset, he had refused to plead, and the second on 23 October 1615 when the threat of torture had made him see reason. Francis Bacon reported that all other legal business in London ground to a halt while Weston's trial continued. Weston was hanged at Tyburn on 25 October. Sir Thomas Monson, who is mentioned in this letter, had appointed both Helwys and Weston and was twice brought for trial himself, but both times proceedings were interrupted. He was later released without being tried.

It was lucky for Simon Forman that he was already dead. The accusations made against him as evidence in the Overbury case would have condemned him to a horrible end. In the year of his death, 1612, he was said to have used wax images to make Carr fall in love with Frances Howard and to secure a lover for Anne Turner, her friend and confidante. Turner's meetings with Forman were also said to involve the devil and, again through wax images, the assassination of Prince Henry.

The Earl and Countess of Somerset were indicted in January 1616 but their trial was delayed until May, which only served to heighten public interest. Inigo Jones, Ben Jonson's partner in creating the court masques, was paid £20 to erect the stages and scaffolding for the trial in Westminster Hall. James' concern with the judgement of 'eternal posterity' has not prevented his interference in the case from being judged harshly.

JAMES WROTE:

First page
Right trusty and well-beloved counsellors, and trusty and well-beloved, we greet you well.

In this weighty and important cause which is now in question, the discovery of the truth whereof so much concerns the glory of God and the honour of our service, we cannot satisfy our own conscience if any course should be left unattempted whereby the foulness of so heinous an act may be laid open to the view of the world; both that thereby the innocent may be cleared and the nocent [guilty] punished, the name of our justice (against the virulent malice of slanderous tongues) both be blessed in this present age and hereafter be recommended to eternal posterity.

We therefore have thought it convenient to require you that, before Weston shall come to his second arraignment, you examine the Countess of Somerset, and after confront him apart with her and Mistress Turner, and if you shall find it convenient, with the Earl himself. And because a servant of ours has this day caused this enclosed paper to be exhibited unto us, whereby he would insinuate that

Second page, shown
Weston at his arraignment did recant all his former examinations (whereunto we give no credit, the contrary being testified by the letters of you, our judges), we do require you, the commissioners, again to take the acknowledgement of Weston's former examinations from his own mouth. And you, the judges, with all convenience to send us your opinion of this paper, that accordingly we may resolve to dispose of him who has caused it to be put in our hand. If, for shortness of time, all these particulars cannot be performed before Monday at two of the clock in the afternoon, then are the judges to prorogue their session until such time as they shall find requisite for the performance of the service.

Our pleasure is that you forbear not to control the Lieutenant of the Tower and Sir Thomas Monson and to proceed against them as justice shall require though they be our servants, as more particularly you shall understand from our cousin the Duke of Lennox, who has received his charge from our own mouth and with whom we have clearly confirmed of all these points.

Added with his Majesty's own hand

We must earnestly require you, as you tender both our conscience and honour, to use all means for the full clearing and manifestation of the verity in this business even though you be not bound in law to do it, so that you do nothing against the law, wherein we must trust to your knowledge and integrities.

Weston at his arraignment did recant all
his former examinations, whereunto wee give
no credditt, the contrary being testified by
the letters of your owne Judges: wee doe require
you the Commissioners againe to take the
acknowledgment of Westons former examinations
from his owne mouth, and you the Judges
whoe are soe well conversant in the opinion
of his papers, that accordingly wee may
resolve to dispose of him, wee have caused
it to be put into our hands: &c. for soemuch
of theis all theise perticulers cannot bee
performed, before munday at two of the
clocke in the afternoone, then are the Judges
to prorogue theire Session, untill such tyme
as they shall finde requisite for the
performance of the service.

Our pleasure is that you forbeare not to
examine the Lieutenant of the Tower, Sr Tho: Munson,
and to provide against them as further shall require,
though they be our servants, as more perticulerly you
shall understand from o' Cosin the Duke of Lennox,
whoe hath revoked his charge from o' owne mouth
wth whom wee have likewise conferred of all theis points.

Added wth his Ma'ties owne hand.

Wee must earnestly require you, as you tender both o' conscience &
honour, to use all meanes, for the full clearing and manifestation of the
verity of this busynes, even though you be not bound by law to
doe it, so that you do nothing against the lawe, wherein wee
must trust to your knowledge & integrity.

Tobacco:
Money and Morality

THE GREAT CONTRACT

James is famous for his hatred of tobacco. What financial use did he make of tobacco and the Virginia colony, which produced it? Why did Cecil's attempt to settle James' finances through his Great Contract with Parliament fail, and how did James support himself without Cecil and without Parliament?

James had been poor in Scotland. The Scottish royal household had been maintained in part by the private finance of its officers, which created a grey area between State and private wealth. A committee of eight finance ministers nicknamed 'The Octavians' had imposed stability temporarily on royal finances in Scotland, but James' English Council never succeeded in doing the same in England. James and his family naturally maintained a larger household than Elizabeth had done, but there were considerable savings from having peace between England and Scotland and with Ireland and Spain. James' new kingdoms were not too poor to support him, so long as the government were able to establish a stable basis for Crown finance.

The generosity James had shown at his accession continued unabated. This has been seen as evidence of the King's financial blindness, finding his income to be greatly increased and imagining it to be infinite. In fact James needed to establish his own networks of patronage in his new kingdom where he commanded few traditional loyalties. His attempt to do so through his favourites was

Red leather metal-studded pouch, inscribed in Latin, containing two silver-mounted clay pipes and a finger-shaped bone tobacco stopper, purported to have once been the property of Sir Walter Raleigh, c. 1617. Raleigh imported Spanish tobacco into England and helped create a market for it by smoking it conspicuously himself. It soon became the habit of the young man of fashion.

perhaps understandable, though corruption and extravagance made matters more difficult. Elizabeth had sometimes needed to raise large sums through Parliament in time of war, but her ordinary expenses could largely be met from Crown revenue; James' could not.

In 1606, in order to raise funds, Cecil used the fellow feeling between Parliament and the Crown after the Gunpowder Plot to secure parliamentary subsidies, but such ad hoc grants of subsidy in the absence of regular taxation were always likely to be insufficient. In an attempt to balance the books, Cecil revived old feudal dues and forgotten debts to the Crown, then offered to compound with Parliament to give the King a set allowance in lieu of all these levies. In this 'Great Contract' of 1610 an annual subsidy of £200,000 would be granted to the Crown in return for the abolition of wardship, purveyances and other sources of revenue to which Parliament objected. The contract failed because it could not be made binding. James would not give up his royal prerogative and be bound in a contract with his subjects, while Parliament was, as usual, suspicious of voting money into the pockets of James' Scottish favourites.

Once this opportunity for agreement had been missed, the arguments between Parliament and the Crown over finance grew more rancorous. James

Portrait of Robert Cecil, by Jean Mosnier. James' most influential statesman until his death, he had a pivotal role in the King's succession and represented continuity with the reign of Elizabeth, something James had grounds to resent. Cecil took on incredible amounts of responsibility in diplomacy, finance and general administration, and while James may at times have resented his dependence on him, others were more straightforwardly jealous.

James' relations with his English Parliament began badly with disagreement over the union of England and Scotland and never really recovered. He regarded it as unwieldy, slow to act and lacking in vision. On a rare occasion when Prince Charles seemed to be more popular with Parliament than the King himself, James warned him with his usual prophetic accuracy that he would come to have his 'bellyful of parliaments'.

blamed Cecil for the failure of the contract. After the 1611 prorogation of Parliament the affectionate if patronizing references to Cecil in James' letters as 'my little beagle' disappear. Cecil died in 1612 and the King took control of fiscal policy, aided by various councillors.

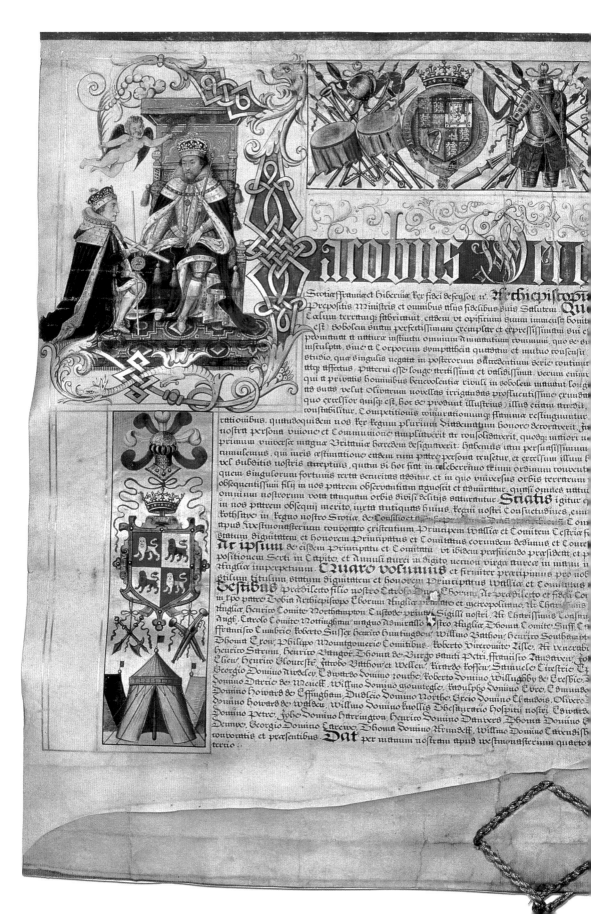

Jacobus

Scotiæ Franciæ et Hiberniæ Rex fidei defensor &c. Archiepiscopis
Præpositis Ministris et omnibus filys fidelibus suis Salutem. Qu...
cælum terramq̃ fabricauit, eidem ut opificium suum immensæ bonit...
est, Sobolem suam perfectissimum exemplar et expressissimum sui...
promittat et natturæ instinctu omnium Animantium communi, quo &c su...
insculptū, sine et Corporum sympathia quædam et mutuo consensu...
studio, quæ singulis negatā in posterorum successentium serie continua...
itaq̃ affectus, Patterni esse longe tertissima et validissima, verum enim...
qui et priuatis hominibus beneuolentiæ riuuli in sobolem uiuunt lon...
tis suas velut Oliuitum nouellas irriguidas profluentissimo erumb...
quo excelsior quisq̃ est, hoc &c produnt illustrius, illud etiam attedit...
constabilitur, Compexitionis uniuerationumq̃ ftiminæ restinguuntur...
rationibus, quibusdoquidem nos Rex regum plurimū distentium honore detorauerit, In...
nostri persona unione et Communione amplitudinem et consolidauerit, In...
primum uniuersæ magnæ Brittaniæ hæredem designauerit: Habemus itatu persuatissimum...
tumulemus, qui iuris æstimatione eidem tum Patris persona trusetur, et excelsum illum b...
vel subditis nostris Acceptius, quam si hoc sint in celeberrimo trium ordinum conuentu...
quem singulorum fortunis tertæ securitas Additur, et in quo uniuersus orbis terrarum...
obsequentissimi fily in nos Patrem obseruantiam Agnoscit et Admiratur, quisit omnes nattur...
omnium nostrorum votis tanquam orbis diuisi delitys satturantur. **Statis** igitur q...
in nos Patrem obsequij merito, iuxta antiquitas huius Regni nostri Consuetudines, eum...
Rothsāye in Regno nostro Scotia, &c Consilio et A... Dati... Com...
Apud Westmonasterium roborato existentium Principem Walliæ et Comitem Cestriæ f...
statuim dignitatem et honorem Principatus et Comitatus eorundem designimus et Coure...
At ipsum &c eisdem Principatu et Comitatu et ibidem præsidendo præsidentt, et p...
positionem Serti in Capite, et Annuli Aurei in digito, uernon virga Aurea in manu u...
Angliæ imperpetuam. **Eūaro volumus** et firmiter præcipimus pro nob...
stilum titulum statum dignitatem et honorem Principatus Walliæ et Comitatus...
Testibus Prædilecto filio nostro Carolo Duci Eborum Angliæ, Ac prædilecto et fideli Co...
in Xpo patre Tobia Archiepiscopo Eborum Angliæ primato et metropolitano, Ac Christissimo...
Angliæ, Henrico Comite Northampton Custode priuati Sigilli nostri, Ac Charissimo Consan...
Angl. Carolo Comite Nottingham magno Admirallo Xtro Angliæ Thoma Comite Suff. C...
ffratruisco Cumbrio Roberto Sussex Henrico Huntingdon Willmo Vitthow henrico Southampt...
Thoma Crow Philippo Mountgomerie Comitibus, Roberto Vicecomiti Zisle, At uenerabi...
Henrico Sarum, Henrico Bangor, Thoma de Burgo statui Petri ffrancisco Assauren... el...
Eliew henrico Glouestr, Jacobo Batthowet Wellen, Rirardo Rossen, Samuele Cirestrio Ch...
Georgio Domino Awdeley, Edwardo Domino Routhe, Roberto Domino Willughby de Eresbio...
Domino Darrio de Meuek, Willmo Domino Mounteagle, Indulpho Domino Ebre, Edmundo...
Domino howard de Effingham, Dudleio Domino Northe, Greio Domino Chandois, Oliuero...
Domino howard de Walden, Willmo Domino Knollis Thesaurario hospity nostri, Edward...
Domino Petre, Joho Domino harrington, henrico Domino Danvers, Thoma Domino E...
Denny, Georgio Domino Carew, Thoma Domino Arundell, Willmo Domino Cauendish...
contouratis et præsentibus **Dat** per manum nostram Apud Westmonasterium quarto...
terio:-

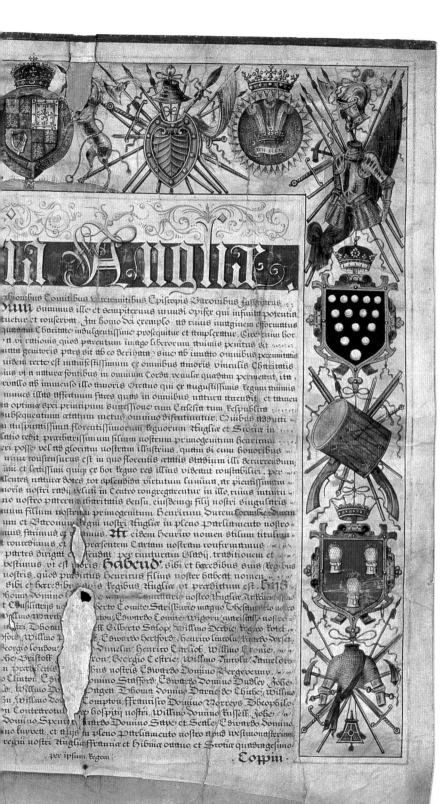

Letters patent creating Prince Henry Prince of Wales and Earl of Chester, dated 4 June 1610. The decorated initial 'J' shows James enthroned, handing the letters patent to Henry. The investiture came soon after the assassination of Henry IV of France, which shattered Prince Henry's dreams of military service with him. Prince Henry surrounded the ceremony with tilts and chivalry, seeking to dignify chivalry above the money grabbing which occupied much of court life. Nonetheless James used the investiture to appeal to Parliament for money to finance Henry in his new role. James was keen that Henry should not appear too regal in his own right and tended to accompany him rather than allow him solitary progresses through London.

James pursued a revenue policy based on widening the scope of existing customs duties on mercantile vested interests, and improving the efficiency of their collection in a way not injurious to the people. The failure of the Great Contract compelled the King to place greater reliance on individual projects and private tax collectors. James received too many different opinions from too many councillors: rival policies abounded and contradicted each other. This was certainly true of the policy on tobacco.

SPAIN, VIRGINIA AND TOBACCO

James' interest in Virginia had waned after the initial charter to the Virginia Company in 1606, as the financial possibilities of the colony appeared limited.

Pocahontas was a nickname bestowed by her father, referring to her playfulness as a child. The inscription gives both her original name, Matoaka, and the name she took at baptism, Rebecca. Her unlikely friendship with Captain Smith and her marriage to John Rolfe helped preserve the early colonists and promote a level of understanding between her people and theirs. She is fashionably dressed and by all accounts enjoyed James' court and the reception she received, but her expedition proved fatal to her health.

A woodcut of pilgrims about to set sail on the *Mayflower*. The founders of New England are pictured fleeing religious persecution, in the form of burning for heresy. James' policy was to export those who could not live within the Church as he defined it, rather than burn them. This put whole groups opposed to his policies beyond his power to control.

Subsequent charters in 1609 and 1612 loosened the Crown's grip on the company. By 1616 the trade in tobacco had revived the Crown's interest. Pocahontas was honoured by James' court and accorded ambassadorial rank in attending a masque as a representative of her father Powhatan. Read a letter from John Chamberlain describing Pocahontas' visit: document 14, *Pocahontas at court*.

The King's view and use of Virginia did not match this gracious reception. It was a place to where religious malcontents, whose execution might have excited popular sympathy, were deported instead. While many feared being sent to America, some began to go voluntarily to escape persecution. Among them was a group of dissenters who made their way to New England in 1620 who became known as the Pilgrim Fathers. This group were financially supported by Edwin Sandys, a manager of the Virginia Company and one of those Parliamentarians who had made legal objections to the proposed union of England and Scotland. Opinions that James' government could not tolerate flourished in Virginia and the promoters of the colony were often those most opposed to James' policies at home.

Pocahontas at court

A letter from John Chamberlain to Sir Dudley Carleton, 22 June 1616. In this letter John Chamberlain, the court intelligencer, reports on the impact of Pocahontas at James' court and makes some prescient remarks about the future of the colony.

James' interest in Virginia revived with the trade in tobacco, despite his hatred of the weed. Sir Thomas Dale came back to London in the spring of 1616, to seek further financial support for the Virginia Company. To ensure spectacular publicity, he brought with him about a dozen Algonquin Indians, including Pocahontas. She had married John Rolfe, a tobacco planter, in 1614. Her husband and their young son, Thomas, accompanied her.

Pocahontas was accorded ambassadorial place as the representative and councillor of her father Powhatan at the twelfth night masque of 1617, Ben Jonson's *Vision of Delight*. This was the same masque which saw Villiers, the newly created Earl of Buckingham, first publicly display his status as chief royal favourite in a dance with the Queen.

In a letter of 18 January 1617 Chamberlain reported Pocahontas was 'on her return (though sore against her will) if the wind would come about to send them away'. In March 1617 they set sail, but it was soon apparent that Pocahontas would not survive the voyage home. She was ill from pneumonia or possibly tuberculosis. She was taken ashore, where she died and was buried in a churchyard at Gravesend. She was 22 years old.

JOHN CHAMBERLAIN WROTE:

The bishop of Winchester came sick from Greenwich on Sunday last, and on Monday night died in Sir Francis Goodwin's house at Westminster. His bishopric was bestowed (or at least promised) the next day to the bishop of Bath and Wells: but who shall succeed in his place is not so soon or easily resolved. Sir Thomas Dale is arrived from Virginia and bought with him some ten or twelve old and young of that country, among whom the most remarkable person is Pocahontas (daughter of Powatan a king or cacique [chief] of that country) married to one Rolfe an English man: I hear not of any other riches or matter of worth, but only some quantity of sassafras [a stimulant], tobacco, pitch and clap-board [wood for making barrels and houses], things of no great value unless there were more plenty and nearer hand. All I can learn of it is that the country is good to live in, if it were stored with people, and might in time become commodious, but there is no present profit to be expected: but you may understand more by yourself when he comes into those parts, which he pretends [says he intends] to do with in a month or little more. Yesterday was sevenight [a week ago yesterday] (which was the last time I saw Master Secretary) I moved [urged] him again for your journey to the Spa. He answered as before that he had heard nothing of it from yourself. I assured him you had written about it, howsoever the letter was miscarried or mislaid. He said he would enquire of Moore and if he found any such thing he would move the King for leave between that and Sunday night. What he has done I know not, for I love not to haunt him at Court without extraordinary occasion. As I was now making an end [to this letter] Dieston brings me your letter of the 15th of this present, which containing no matter that requires answer I will here conclude with all due remembrance to my Lady and so commend you to the protection of the Almighty. From London this 22nd of June 1616. Your Lordship's to command, John Chamberlain…

the bishop of winchester came ficke from Greenwich on
funday last, and on monday night died in S.r Fraunces
Goodwins house at westminster, his bishopricke was
bestowed (or at least promised) the next day to the
bishop of Bath and wells: but who shall succeed in
his place is not fo foone nor eafilier refolved. S.r Tho=
mas Dale is arrived from virginia and brought
w.th him fome ten or twelue old and younge of that
countrie, among whom the most remarqueable perfon
is Poca-huntas (daughter to Powatan a kinge or
cacique of that countrie) maried to one Rolfe an
english man: I heare not of any other riches or mat=
ter of worth, but only fome quantitie of faffafras to=
bacco pitch and clap-boord, things of no great value
vnles there were more plentie and nearer hand
all I can learne of yt is that the countrie is goode to
liue in, yf yt were ftored w.th people, and might in time
become commodious, but there is no prefent profit to
be expected: but you may vnderstand more by
himfelf when he comes into thofe parts, w.ch he pretends
to do w.th in a moneth or litle more. yesterday was
feuennight (w.ch was the last time I faw m.r Secretarie)
moued him again for y.r iourny to the Spa, he aunfwe=
red as before that he had heard nothing of yt from
yo.rfelf, I assured him you had written about yt how=
foever the letter was mifcaried or miflayed, he faide
he would inquire of moore, and yf he found any fuch
thing he wold moue the king for leaue twixt that and
funday night, what he hath don I know not, for I haue
not to haunt him at court w.thout fome extraordinarie
occafion. as I was now making an end Buckner
bringes me yo.r letter of the 25.th of this prefent
w.ch contemning no matter that requires aunfwer
I will here conclude w.th all due remembrance to
my Lady and fo commend you to the protection of
the Almighty. From london this 22.th of June 1616

yo.r L.ps to command
John Chamberlain

To M.r Chamberlain
22 of June
1616

Map of Virginia. Powhatan's court is described in the same terms as James' own: 'Powhatan held this state and fashion when Capt. Smith was delivered to him prisoner'. The limitations of the map are frankly confessed in the key 'to the Crosses has been discovered, what is beyond is by relation'. The Virginians themselves presented an image too appealingly exotic to be overlooked, and they soon began to be represented in the masque.

James' dislike of tobacco was genuine. Some said he disliked it because Sir Walter Raleigh had imported it, or that he disliked Raleigh for introducing it. As with religion and witchcraft James was prepared to set out his opinions in print. His famous *Counterblaste* was part of a pamphlet war about the medicinal properties of the drug. Sir John Beaumont's *Metamorphosis of Tobacco* claimed that it healed quarrels and made you lucky in love. This poem was a financial success for John Flasket in 1602, and this cannot have endeared him to the King in Star Chamber. James encouraged an alternative market in domestic silk, but the silkworms tended to die en route.

After the lapse of its rights under charter the Virginia Company was granted a monopoly in the tobacco trade in return for a large additional customs payment of 6d per pound weight to the Crown. The cultivation and sale of domestic tobacco was outlawed. Almost immediately Lionel Cranfield, James' financial adviser with a background in and clear understanding of trade, struck a better deal. This granted a fresh monopoly on the whole trade to Sir Thomas Roe in exchange for an annual rent of £16,000. This allowed the importation of cheap Spanish tobacco to the detriment of the colonial product. Against this background, in July 1620, came one of

15 *Noisome weed*

Proclamation restraining the disorderly trade in tobacco, 29 June 1620. After the elaborate moral and medical preamble of the proclamation it becomes clear that the measure is fundamentally about money, and the new monopoly in the trade.

The document betrays something of the struggle in the minds of the government between the possible financial benefits to the Crown of the custom on tobacco and James' personal dislike of the weed. There is tension too between the apparent severity of the law and the apparent ineffectiveness of previous measures of a similar kind. There appears to be a gulf between the theoretical and actual power of the Crown in governing trade. Government by proclamation, enforcing a proclamation acknowledged to be ineffective by issuing another proclamation, looks rather more hopeful than pragmatic.

It is debatable whether Sir Walter Raleigh or James himself did more to advertise tobacco: one by smoking it conspicuously, the other by fulminating against its harmful properties. James' medical knowledge mixed acute common sense observations with the learned non-sense of the time. James did make one decisive if perhaps unwitting contribution to medicine by freeing the Apothecaries' Company from the Grocers, a major step in the evolution of the modern medical profession.

The Virginia Company felt betrayed by the measures, which threatened the commercial survival of the colony. It petitioned James to 'restore to us our ancient liberty or otherwise to send us all home'. This appeal to 'ancient liberty', rather ridiculous in the case of a company as new as the Virginia Company, was the characteristic language of Parliament in upholding the precedents of the Common Law against the innovations of Royal Prerogative, and underlines the role of the company in the group opposed to James' policy.

There were many more twists in tobacco policy. James soon dissolved the Virginia Company, a step towards a final admission that all he could do was let the merchants run it themselves without royal interference. It has also been seen as an attack on Edwin Sandys, the Virginia Company manager and friend of the Pilgrim Fathers, whom James compared unfavourably to the devil. After the failure of the Spanish marriage in 1624, Spanish tobacco was banned once more.

THE PROCLAMATION READS:

...Whereas We, out of the dislike We had of the use of Tobacco, tending to a general and new corruption both of men's bodies and manners, and yet nevertheless holding it of the two more tolerable, that the same should be imported amongst many other vanities and superfluities, which came from beyond the Seas, than permitted to be planted here within this Realm, thereby to abuse and misemploy the soil of this fruitful Kingdom, did by our Proclamation dated the thirtieth day of December now last past, straitly [strictly] charge and command all and every person and persons, of what degree or position soever, That they or any of them by themselves, their servants, workmen or labourers, should not from and after the second day of February then next following, presume to sow, set or plant, or cause to be sown, set or planted within this Our Realm of England and the Dominion of Wales, any sort or kind of Tobacco whatsoever, and that they, or any of them, should not maintain or continue any old stocks or plants of Tobacco formerly sown or planted, but should forthwith utterly destroy and root up the same. And whereas We have taken into Our Royal consideration as well the great waste and consumption of the wealth of Our Kingdoms, as the endangering and impairing the health of Our Subjects, by the inordinate liberty and abuse of Tobacco, being a weed of no necessary use, and but of late years brought in to Our Dominions, and being credibly informed, that divers Tobacconists, and other mean persons taking upon them to trade and adventure into the parts beyond the Seas for Tobacco, to the intent to forestall and engross the said commodity upon unmerchantlike conditions, do transport much Gold bullion and coin out of Our Kingdoms, and do barter and vend the Staple commodities of our Realm at under-values, to the intent to buy Tobacco, to the discredit of Our

Second membrane

native merchandizes, and extreme enhancing of the rates and prices of Tobacco, and the great disturbance and decay of the Trade of the orderly and good merchant. We taking the premises into Our Princely consideration, and being desirous to put a remedy to the said inconveniences, which We have long endeavoured, though with less effect than We expected, have resolved to make some further redress, by restraining the disordered traffic in that Commodity, and reducing it into the hands of able persons that may manage the same without inconvenience, whereby the general abuse may be taken away, and the necessary use (if any be) may be preserved. We do therefore ... by these presents, straitly charge and command, that Our said Proclamation restraining the planting of Tobacco, be in every respect observed and performed according to the tenor thereof, upon the penalties therein contained...

The which we out of the dislike we had of the use of Tobacco tending to a generall and noe corrupton both of mens bodies and mindes and yet neverthelesse houlding it of the three more tollerable that the same should be imported amongest many other vertuous and unplentifull Earth thence from beyond the Seas then planted to be planted here within this Realme and thereby to abuse and misimploy the soile of this fruitfull Kingdome did by our Proclamation dated the thirtieth day of December nowe last past streightly thing and commaund all and everie person and persons of what degree or condition soever that they or any of them by themselves they servauntes workmen or labourers should not from and after the second day of ffebruarie then next following presume to sowe sett or plant or cause to be sowen sett or planted within this our Realme of England and the Dominion of Wales any sort or kinde of Tobacco whatsoever and that they or any of them shold not mayntayne or contynue any old stockes or plantes of Tobacco formerly sowen or planted but shold forthwith utterly destroy and roote up the same And Whereas we have taken into our serious consideration aswell the greate waste and consumpton of the Wealth of our Kingdomes and the endangering and impayring of the health of our Subiectes by the inordinate libty and abuse of Tobacco beinge a Weede of noe necessarie use and but of little profit brought into our Dominions and being redilly informed that divers Tobacconistes and other meane persons takeing upon them to trade and adventure into the partes beyond the Seas for Tobacco to the intent to forestall and ingrosse the said comodity upon unmerchantlike conditions doe thereby transport much gould bullion and Coyne out of our kingdomes and doe barter and vent the staple comodities of our Realme att under valewes to the intent to buy Tobacco to the disherritt of our

inside notwithstandinge and extreame enhaunsing of the rates and prizes of Tobacco and the greate disturbance and decay of the trade of the orderly and good merchant We takeinge the premisses into our Princely consideration and being desirous to put a remedy to the said inconveniences Which we have long endevoured though with lesse effect then we expected have resolved to make some further redresse by restrayning the disordered traffique in that comodity and reduceing it into the handes of able persons that may mayntayne the same without inconvenience Whereby the generall abuse may be taken away and the necessarie use if any be may be preserved wee doe therefore not onely by these presentes streightly thing and commaund That our said Proclamation restrayning the planting of Tobacco be in everie respect observed and performed according to the tenor thereof upon the penalties therein contayned but alsoe that noe person or persons whatsoever Englishmen denizens or straungers other then such as shalbe authorized and apointed thereunto by letters Pattent under our greate Seale of England doe import or cause to be imported into this our Realme of England or Dominion of Wales or any part of them or either of them any Tobacco of what nature kinde or sort soever after the tenth day of July next ensuing the date hereof from any the partes beyond the Seas upon pane of forfeiture to us of all such Tobacco soe to be imported contrary to the true meaning of these presentes

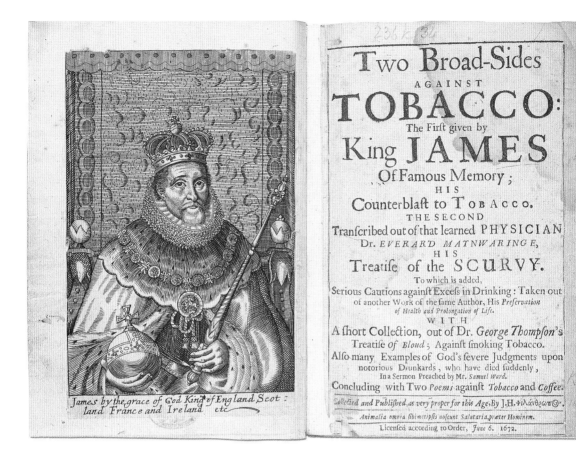

Two Broad-Sides
AGAINST
TOBACCO:
The First given by
King JAMES
Of Famous Memory;
HIS
Counterblaft to TOBACCO.
THE SECOND
Tranfcribed out of that learned PHYSICIAN
Dr. *EVERARD MATNWARINGE*,
HIS
Treatife of the SCURVY.
To which is added,
Serious Cautions againft Excefs in Drinking: Taken out
of another Work of the fame Author, His *Prefervation
of Health and Prolongation of Life.*
WITH
A fhort Collection, out of Dr. *George Thompfon's*
Treatife *of Bloud*; Againft fmoking Tobacco.
Alfo many Examples of God's fevere Judgments upon
notorious Drunkards, who have died fuddenly,
In a Sermon Preached by Mr. *Samuel Ward.*
Concluding with Two *Poems* againft *Tobacco* and *Coffee.*
Collected and Publifhed, as very proper for this Age, By J.H. ΦιΛανθρωπ⊙·.
Animalia omnia fibi mettipfis nofcunt Salutaria, præter Hominem.
Licenfed according to Order, *June* 6. 1672.

James by the grace of God King of England Scotland France and Ireland etc

Frontispiece to *Two Broadsides Against Tobacco*. This image of 'James the wise' lends tone and authority to this volume of 1672 incorporating later thinking on the ill effects of tobacco. By the date of this edition James' tracts themselves had begun to look dated. His mixture of biblical and classical erudition is beginning to be joined and superseded by the experimental work of practising physicians.

a series of proclamations with which James attempted to regulate the trade in tobacco. Like modern tobacco legislation it cloaks financial self-interest in moral superiority; read document 15, *Noisome weed*.

Attempts to regulate the trade in tobacco by proclamation were predictably ineffective. Enforcement through Star Chamber of the monopolies which they proclaimed was exemplary and occasional rather than comprehensive, but the perception of these measures was often negative within court circles as well as outside. Monopolies were nothing new. Elizabeth had granted them to, among others, Sir Walter Raleigh – one of the reasons why he was unpopular. In principle they were sensible measures, which

Sir Walter Raleigh (miniature). Once the jewel of Elizabeth's court, Raleigh spent years under James imprisoned in the Tower, a figurehead for contemporary malcontents and an exemplary victim of tyrannous monarchical oppression for a later generation of opponents of the Stuarts. Many of his later adherents would have recoiled from the arrogant, courtier monopolist of this portrait.

guaranteed income to the Crown while leaving the difficult business of revenue collection to private individuals. However the number of monopolies, the speed with which they were granted, and especially the way they appeared to contradict each other helped create the appearance of a government lacking in direction and one whose instruments were self-seeking and corrupt. The use of Star Chamber as a fiscal instrument, enforcing financially motivated proclamations and generating revenue itself through fines, reinforced this perception. Read a contemporary account of the use of the Star Chamber to enforce the tobacco monopoly in document 16, *The 'world terrified'*.

Recalling Parliament in 1621 James told MPs they could no longer cite mismanagement as a reason not to grant him money, but by then the monopolies themselves had become a sticking point. There was still no settlement of Crown finance. The Monopolies Bill ended Star Chamber's power to enforce proclaimed monopolies; Parliament was rightly sceptical of James' ability and desire to reform abuses of monopolies he had established through Villiers as part of his network of patronage. Charles I later revived these powers.

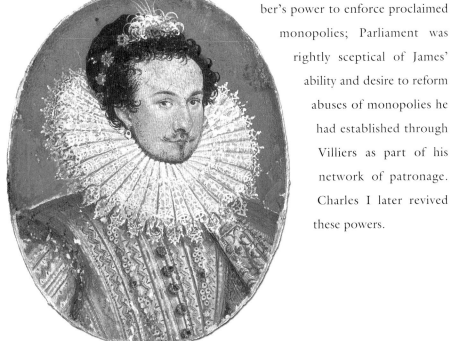

The 'world terrified'

A letter from John Chamberlain, the court intelligencer, to Sir Dudley Carleton, 8 July 1620. This letter shows Chamberlain's reaction to the tobacco monopoly proclaimed and underwritten in document 15. It also attempts to gauge some of the wider reaction to the way the tobacco monopoly worked and was enforced through the court of Star Chamber.

Fittingly the letter also mentions apparent corruption among the officers of Star Chamber themselves in arresting Catholic priests and then letting them go in return for money. The particular instances Chamberlain discusses begin to read like a general account of malaise in the government. The extent to which the business of government was still attendant on the King's person is clear from Chamberlain's remarks about James' absence. Because of disease and a growing disenchantment, the King's absences were becoming more frequent and prolonged.

The letter also illustrates the growing influence of the Spanish ambassador, who knows the strength of the English force sent to defend the Palatinate against Spain and jokes about it. The cause of James' son-in-law Frederick was an appealing one to popular Protestantism, but it is evident there are not many volunteers to defend the Palatinate, perhaps because the aims of the force were not clear and because there was a general lack of confidence in those in authority. After months of prevarication James had finally committed troops to the Protestant cause in Europe but the action lacked any real conviction or momentum. The campaign failed to gain the King real popularity because his motives and degree of commitment were suspected.

In September 1619 Chamberlain reported that the tobacco monopolist Sir Thomas Roe had returned rich from the East Indies, and in October that he had been with James at Hampton Court and had presented him with two antelopes, 'a strange and beautiful kind of red deer'. Chamberlain was unsure how much of this was Roe's personal property and how much belonged to the East India Company.

THE LETTER READS:

My very good Lord: I wrote last week by Dieston, and if Harman had not now called upon me I should scant have thought upon writing, having so little to send. Our ambassadors are all despatched and gone, as well Sir Harry Wootton as Sir Edward Conway and Sir Richard Weston, and Sir John Merrick this day sevenight [a week ago]. Sir Henry Wootton is so confident of himself and his dexterity in managing the business he goes about that he told divers [several] of our captains he was in hope to effect that they should keep their swords in their scabbards: in the mean time our new levies go on but heavily, and whereas they thought they should have been oppressed with multitudes of followers, they are fain [obliged] to send far and near into the country to make up their numbers, which if they were once full they would be gone presently this next week. I am sorry Sir Horace Vere should go so slenderly accompanied as to command but 2000 men, which gives the Spanish ambassador occasion to break jests, and say he must confess we are a very brave nation that dare adventure with 2000 to encounter 10000. The King is now about Oatlands and Windsor but expected here this day or tomorrow. The progress begins the 18th day of this month, and then we are likely to have little to do, seeing this last term is passed over without any remarkable matter, more than the censuring of a pursuivant [attendant] in the Star Chamber for making a traffic of taking priests and letting them go for money: and there was another fellow expected for giving out everywhere and openly that before Michaelmas we should have toleration of religion: indeed the world is now much terrified with the Star Chamber, there being not so little an offence against any proclamation but is liable and subject to the censure of that court.

The letter continues:

And for proclamations and patents they are become so ordinary, that there is no end, every day bringing forth some new project or other, as within these two days here is one come forth for tobacco wholly ingrossed [monopolized] by Sir Thomas Roe and his partners, which if they can keep and maintain against the general clamour, will be a matter of great commodity, unless peradventure [by chance] indignation (rather than all other reasons) may bring that filthy weed out of use. In truth the world does groan under the burden of these perpetual patents, which are become so frequent, that whereas at the King's coming in there were complaints of some eight or nine monopolies then in being, they are now said to be multiplied to so many scores…

My very goode Lord: I wrote the last
weeke by Liston, and yf Harman had not
now called upon me I shold scant have
thought upon writing having so litle to send.
our ambassaders are all dispatcht and gon,
as well Sr Harry Wotton as Sr Edward
Conway and Sr Richard Weston, and Sr
John Merricke this day sevenight. Sr Henry
Wotton is so confident of himself and his
dexteritie in managing the busines he goes
about that he told divers of our capptaines he
was in hope & effect that they shold kepe their
swords in theyre scabberds: in the mean time
our new levies go on but heavilie, and wheras
they thought they shold have ben oppressed wth
multitudes of followers, they are faine to send
far and neere into the countrie to make vp
theyre numbers, wch yf they were once full
they wold be gon presently this next weeke.
I am sory Sr Horace Vere shold go so slenderly
accompanied as to command but 2000 men,
wch gives the Spanish ambassader occasion
to breake iests, and says he must needs
confesse we are a very brave nation that
dare adventure wth 2000 to incounter 10000.
The King is now about Otelands and Windsor
but expected here this day or to morow, the
progresse begins the 18th of this moneth, and
then we are like to have litle to do, seeing
this last terme is past over wthout any re=
marckable matter, more then the censuring
of a pursevant in the star-chamber for making
a trafficke of taking priests and letting them
go for monie: and there was another fellow
expected for giving out openly and every
where that before Michaelmas we shold have
toleration of religion: indeed the world is now
much terrified wth the star-chamber, there being
not so litle an offence against any proclamation
but is liable and subiect to the censure of that
court.

'Blessed are the Peacemakers'

ROYAL DIPLOMACY: MASQUE AND REALITY

Blessed are the Peacemakers' was James' motto. His peaceful foreign policy has largely been seen as successful in Scotland, but generally as a failure in England, where it dominated the final years of his reign. More than in domestic policy there were factors in foreign affairs that the King could not control.

The King attempted to exert control over foreign policy through the marriage treaties of his children. This was a return to the normal course of European diplomacy. Queen Elizabeth, childless and unmarried, had played the marriage game with the great powers of Europe for as long as she credibly could, and then concentrated on extending England's wealth and influence without marriage beyond Europe through sea power. James sought to rebalance the powers in Europe through the treaty with Spain and to negotiate the best terms he could with the great powers through his children.

One of Inigo Jones' elaborate Italianate designs for the *Lords Masque* of 1613, one of the many festivities surrounding the marriage of Princess Elizabeth to the Elector Palatine.

His own marriage to the house of Denmark had placed James in alliance with it and with allied Protestant powers, though Queen Anne's conversion to Catholicism soon after her arrival in Scotland was something of an embarrassment. Negotiations for a marriage between one of James' sons and a Spanish princess, to cement the treaty with Spain, spanned the length of James' reign. Around the time of the Spanish treaty, with the Spanish ambassador the favoured guest of the masque, both sides made diplomatic moves towards a marriage, but there were obstacles. Spain insisted on the conversion of the English groom to Catholicism. There were domestic objections too. James underestimated the popular identification of the English with Elizabeth's anti-Spanish foreign policy.

Ratification of the Anglo-Spanish treaty by Philip, King of Spain, Valladolid, 1605. James preserved this treaty and the hope of a Spanish match for Henry and then Charles for nearly 20 years. When this treaty was finally revoked it was replaced by a treaty with France which was no more popular in the country and which deprived James and his successors of any influence they may have had with Spain over issues like the Palatinate.

Britain, unlike Scotland alone, could not avoid the power struggles of Europe without losing credibility and this, in practice, meant siding against Spain. There was also the indifference of English merchants, driving colonial expansion in New World territory claimed by Spain, to royal proclamations and treaties.

Partly out of a genuine hatred of piracy and partly to please Spain, James recalled the letters of marque Elizabeth had granted to privateers. This had the opposite effect to the one he intended. Removing royal sanction also removed the last vestige of royal control. Piracy boomed. The Crown could control neither the pirates nor the trade they preyed upon, as merchants across continents seemed able to circumvent both treaty and proclamation. Despite the Virginia Company's charters and the royal name of the early settlement at Jamestown, Virginia was not a royal undertaking or governed by courtly diplomacy. James could entertain Pocahontas at court but the real business of Virginia was done through the managers of the Company.

There were symbolic attempts to embrace mercantile subjects in the court masque. Ben Jonson's masque written for the opening of Cecil's New Exchange, later the Royal Exchange, in 1609 has recently come to light in the National Archives. It is full of conventional praise for the monarch, but has something of his great stage play *Bartholomew Fair* about it; a play in which the scale and profusion of commercial activity is beyond the power of the law to control. Read an extract from Jonson's masque in document 17, *The masque of monarchy*.

GOVERNING AT A DISTANCE: IRELAND AND SCOTLAND

Before 1603 James had 'planted' people in distant parts of his kingdom in an attempt to exert royal authority and bring increased customs income to the Crown. Gentlemen farmers from Fife were planted on the Isle of Lewis and though that enterprise had failed James considered that a similar experiment in Ulster would be more successful.

As King of Scotland James had pursued his usual balanced policy with regard to Ireland, negotiating with Hugh O'Neill, Earl of Tyrone in his rebellion against the English while issuing proclamations against him to win favour with Elizabeth. Despite the miraculous delaying rhetoric, still celebrated in Ireland, of Cormack McCarthy, Lord of Blarney, Elizabeth's general in Ireland Charles Blount, Lord Mountjoy had delivered to the dying Elizabeth an advantageous end of the war in Ireland. The Earls of Tyrone and Tyrconnel sought Spanish help in 1607 generating tales of a drunken odyssey across the Catholic states

Verses from Ben Jonson's *The Key Keeper. A Masque for the Opening of Britain's Burse*, 19 April 1609. This masque was discovered in 1996 among the State Papers and celebrates the opening of a lavish and fashionable market. The verses shown here are elaborately laudatory as befits a courtly entertainment. The masque reached its zenith under Jonson and Inigo Jones late in James' reign but, though used to flattery, James was rather bored by its decorousness. He preferred the anti-masque, developed by Jonson: a comic beginning showing grotesques and disorders, which are then overcome in the harmony of the masque itself.

This masque mixes decorousness, in the verses, with the chaotic element, which James found more entertaining, in prose. The source of the chaos is the overwhelming and overflowing market itself, which almost defies description let alone control. The masque shares this theme with Jonson's great stage play *Bartholomew Fair* (1614). James' government tried several times to ban the real Bartholomew Fair ostensibly for the risk of spreading plague among the crowds that gathered there, but also because of the lawlessness which went with it. Attempts to curb the excesses of the fair in the play end in ridicule, satire perhaps aimed at attempts by James' government to control trade by proclamation. This masque is full of the new high fashion for all things Chinese, while *Bartholomew Fair* concentrates on lower status items, but the language of the Shop Boy in the masque and Leatherhead in the play is very similar.

Shop Boy: What do you lack? What is't you buy? Very fine china glasses of all kinds and qualities? China chains, China bracelets, China scarves, China fans, China girdles, China knives...'

The Key Keeper

Leatherhead: What do you lack, Gentlemen? What is it you buy? Fine Rattles? Drums? Babies? Little Dogs? and Birds for Ladies? What do you lack?

Bartholomew Fair

Needless to say the stall-holders in *Bartholomew Fair* smoke fiendishly.

THE VERSES READ:

If to your ear it wonder being
To hear Apollo's statue sing
'Gainst nature's law
Ask this great King

And his fair Queen, who are the proper cause
It is not wisdom's power alone
Or Beauty's that can more astound
But both so high
In this great King

And his fair Queen do strike the harmony
Which harmony has power to touch
The dullest earth and make it such
As I am now
To this great King

And his fair Queen, whom none to praise knows how
Except with silence which indeed
Does truest admiration breed
And that can I
To this best King
And his best Queen in my last note and die...

if it wase eare it wondes being
to heer Apollos salves singe
Earthe natures lawe
Like the great kinge

And his faier Queene, whose awfull graces ranke
yf it not wisdomes power alone
or Beauties but rare manners showe,
But both so hyghe
Makt great kinge

And his faier Queene do strike the humour
while humour guts growes to toune
The Dullest earth, and makes it furs

As I am nowe
To his great kinge

And his faier Queene, whose none to praise knowes how
Excepte in silence where indeed
Doth truste admiration breed
And that same I
To his beste kinge

And his beste Queene in an last note I dye.

I would my Antagonist at Eltham was hes nowe to heare
what he would say, the his is past the heat of sande, or the beames
of the sunne, well said looke like a man that would gone good
far off, I say like it Instantly I am going south
for verginia to discover the Inforta of that countrey, the
kind of Aly the hane not, and so doer land for Virginia: to
tompare the astronomid, and but soe whose parade did
stood, and being of the birde alive spine, where hapes I will
call upon my selfe by the way. if he will gone me
up for one at an returne, tis good, Hee make no feire
wih yt, a man shall valewe it, Hee send it yf I come, And
madam let me have a mache with yt two, heere a picture
that I doe valewe at some thing, but for the mates, and that
while spreade it, the workman like, yf it the salutation of
the blessed virgin by the Angell gabriel, wih the quier of
other angeles applanding it, this is my selfe I wonder
wih yt, upon the same toaemes, yt looke like a good custome
two, and a good parend too boot I must fitt yd in some sort O
and that was a Bushelsne nowe, what wont not an Alexander
gone for his, it is the whole freind was see a speff, and so a good
horse indeed, I so youe upon the same mache yf yf hor be a
snowres or beantyes other spes, that will like an tale of me, I
will aske no other service but her good woorde, and so yet
handsloes, And god make me his, wih is the sollede prayer
over was and wilbe. I

of Europe, but Spain was no longer in a position to devote resources to foment rebellion. The Earls never returned and their lands came to James.

The King was presented with a number of schemes for dividing the land. He chose the option least favourable to the Irish themselves. James regarded the plantation of settlers in Ulster as both financially and morally superior to imperial rule, and the endowments of land he gave to Protestant educational and religious institutions were intended as a means of supplanting Catholicism in Ireland. This was a far-fetched expectation, especially since James' encouraging overtures to Catholics before 1603 had raised expectations in Ireland that he himself would become Catholic. Needless to say his personal satisfaction with the project was not shared in Ireland. Read James' opinion of the Ulster plantation: document 18, *Pious work*.

Map of Ulster (c. 1609). Happy to cultivate the rebellious Irish lords when they rebelled against Elizabeth, James did not extend his patronage to their followers when the lords left Ulster. As he had done in the Scottish islands, James planned to plant men 'well affected in religion' to work the land and create revenue for the Crown. In Ulster James planned a society governed by English land law, which would establish an English-style gentry, and smallholding class who would bring their religion to supplant Catholicism.

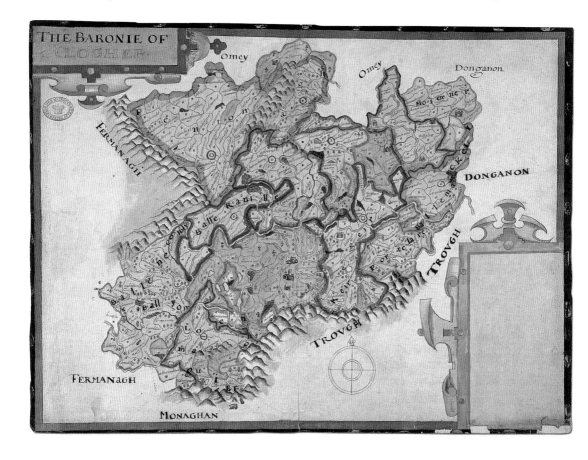

James crammed his sole Irish Parliament with specially created Protestant MPs but it broke up in rancour in 1615, and was not reconvened. Thereafter, he governed Ireland by prerogative without Parliament. By contrast, James famously said that Scotland he was able to 'govern with my pen', in a speech designed to show the English that his supposedly barbarous northern kingdom was more readily governable than his southern one. He governed Scotland through a handful of Privy Councillors and the business of the Scottish Parliament was handpicked and sifted by royal appointees, the Lords of the Articles.

Rather than imposing Scottish institutions on England as his English Parliament had feared, James was more inclined to impose English institutions on the Scots. His only return to Scotland, in 1617, came with an agenda to impose Anglican services. Though the Stuarts had always fancied themselves as European statesmen, as monarchs in Scotland they had always had the option of watching continental conflict from the periphery. James attempted to maintain good relations with Protestant states, anti-Spanish Catholic states and with Spain itself, but the outbreak of war in Europe in 1618 put pressure on James' balanced foreign policy and hindered his attempt to be a king of Christian unity. James hoped a Spanish marriage for one of his sons and Protestant match for his daughter would bring the two sides together.

THE PALATINATE AND SPAIN

The Protestant marriage came in 1613 between Princess Elizabeth and Frederick, Elector Palatine. The match was popular and lavishly celebrated but made James' attempts to act as the peacemaker in Europe much more difficult. Frederick accepted the Crown of Bohemia after the deposition of the Archduke Ferdinand and set himself against the Catholic Imperial Powers and Spain. Frederick was defeated at the Battle of the White Mountain in November 1620, and fled. The doomed romantic plight of the couple made them the darlings of popular Protestantism, but Elizabeth's pleas for help to her father

18   *Pious work*

A clerk's copy of a letter from James to the Irish commissioners in Ulster, 1609 (exact date unknown). This letter directs James' Irish commissioners to accept a greatly increased workload and makes a case for government in Ireland at one remove, rather than directly through the King and Council. The document presents this as a sign of the government's determination to establish well-qualified people as a means of access to royal justice for Irish suitors, but it could also be interpreted as Council and King not wanting to be bothered with such suits directly.

During the Irish rebellions of Elizabeth's reign the greatest resistance to the English and the most prominent insurgent Irish lords had been in Ulster. James had regarded the departure of the rebellious Earls of Tyrone and Tyrconnel on their mission to Spain as an act of defiance, but when their lands fell to the Crown he saw an opportunity to evict the Irish and replace them with English and Scottish settlers. James saw the plantation of Ulster as both practically and morally superior to imperial rule and saw his decision to sell the land 'at undervalues' as an example of his largess in the interests of bringing in 'civil men well-affected in religion'. There were other motives too. The plan he adopted for the plantation of Ulster was a way of paying suitors without dipping into existing Crown revenues. By selling the land under English land tenure he hoped to encourage a class of small landowners and gentry, which would break the power of the Irish chiefs.

James' satisfaction with project did not last long. Those undertaking the plantation recruited Irish labour rather than bringing their own, thereby undermining the intended eviction of the Irish, which was, James admits, 'the fundamental reason of that plantation'.

THE LETTER READS:

Trusty

Forasmuch as we consider and observe that the Plantation in Ulster, as it is a work of piety and honour, so it must be attended with so constant a care and direction both here and there, as it will be necessary to establish some persons of integrity and experience in this kingdom to whom all those that shall be interested therein may ordinarily address themselves, for many things that are incident to the same, being of such nature as are more fit for other men's examination and consideration than for our Privy Council, whom, in regard to their great employments we are desirous to spare from those things which are not of such difficulty and consequence as may not be conveniently done without them. We have made choice of you in respect of our experience of your integrity and sufficiency, to take particular care and notice of all such persons as shall have any occasion to address themselves to us, or to our Council for answer or direction, not only in things which

Second page
have relation to the Plantation aforesaid (wherein you have already taken so great care and pains) but in such other private suits and causes concerning that Kingdom (where every one of you have borne particular place and office) as shall be referred to you from us, or our Privy Council.

Trustee

32

Fforasmuch as wee consid^r & observe that the Plantation
in Ulster, as it is a worke of pietie & honor, so it
must be attended wth so constant a care, & direction, both
here & there, as it wilbe necessary to establish some
persons of integritie, & experience in this king dome,
to whome all those that shalbe interested therein may
ordinarily address them selfs for many things that
are incident to the same being of such nature, as are
more fitt for other mens examination & consideration,
then for our privy Counsell whome, in regard of
their great Imployments, we are desirous to spare from
those things, wch are not of any such difficultie, and consequence, as may not be conveniently done wthout them.
We haue made choyse of you, in respect of our experience
of y^{or} Integritie & sufficiency, to take particular
care, & notice of all such persons, as shall haue any
occasion to address them selfs to vs, or our Councell
for answere, or direction, not only in things w^{ch}

were unavailing. James was unwilling to condone what he saw as Frederick's act of rebellion and came to view popular feeling against Spain as seditious.

Another victim of James' attempt to maintain a balanced foreign policy was Sir Walter Raleigh, imprisoned since his implication in the plots of 1603 and the subject of a show trial and a theatrical reprieve from execution. He was released for an expedition to the Orinoco to search for gold mines. Raleigh's expedition would enrich the Crown if it succeeded, but James reserved the right to disown it if it failed or if it brought Raleigh into conflict with the Spaniards, who claimed the area of the supposed mines for themselves. The odds were stacked against him from the beginning, and, to add to his grief, his crew were ravaged by sickness and his son was killed. Raleigh returned in disgrace to a certain death. Read a contemporary account of Raleigh's death and the last poem he ever wrote in document 19, *Sharp medicine*.

A modern reconstruction of Raleigh's bedchamber in the Tower of London. Before his execution in 1618, Raleigh composed a vigorous defence of his actions here as well as his valedictory verses, though he knew his fate was sealed. Then as now prisoners managed to get themselves published. Raleigh's *History of the World* established his reputation as a martyr of tyranny, the circumstances of its composition contributing to its popularity.

Raleigh's execution is a highly emotive moment in James' reign. Contemporary accounts of his death and his own verses began an immediate cult of Raleigh, which persists even today. He had not been idle in the Tower. His *History of the World*, published in 1614 despite the attempts of James to suppress it, drew the lesson that God punished the wickedness of Princes and that rebellion naturally followed oppression. In the struggle between Charles I and Parliament, Raleigh, the monopolist and courtier, became a hero of the parliamentarians. At the time of his death the court marvelled at his folly and gossiped of his treachery as much as the people admired his heroism.

The protracted marriage negotiations with Spain, first for Prince Henry then after his death in 1612 for Prince Charles, saw a gradual diminution of James' influence with the Protestant states to whom he gave verbal but little practical support. At the same time the influence of the Spanish ambassador on James increased and he began to have as much access to the King as many of the Council. Parliament opposed the Spanish marriage, and in the journal of the House of Commons they recorded their right to speak freely within the House on all matters of State. James tore the declaration out and, on the ambassador's insistence, dissolved Parliament on 30 December 1621, forbidding it to interfere in foreign policy, including royal marriages.

James receiving Charles after the Spanish expedition. The joy and relief of their reunion, accompanied by the celebratory ringing of bells shown here, was short-lived.

Parliament's failure in 1621 to grant James money only made the Spanish match more likely as the King needed to seek alternative sources of revenue. Fearing the popular outcry, and deciding it could only be stifled by a *fait accompli*, Villiers and Prince Charles set out under assumed names (Tom and Jack Smith) to go to Spain and bring back Charles' bride. The pair had a variety of picaresque adventures, which delayed their letters to the King. This terrified James, and not just on a personal level; given his own failing health, the death of his eldest son and now the possibility of Charles falling victim to brigands or treachery in Spain, the secure dynasty he had brought in 1603 hung by a thread. James blamed Villiers for persuading him to let Charles go, but the scheme was the King's own conducted through him in private packets of letters without the knowledge of Parliament or the Council. The rather unexpected consequence of the secret mission to Spain, when the pair returned in failure and humiliation, was that Villiers and eventually

Sharp medicine

An account of the final speech and death of Sir Walter Raleigh, and the verses he wrote on the morning of his execution, 29 October 1618.

Sir Walter Raleigh had almost been executed before; he had gone through the whole process minus the final act in 1603. His theatrical reprieve at the last moment at Winchester had been stage managed by the King. Now, after the failure of the Guiana expedition, there was no hope of reprieve and he stage managed his actual execution himself. His well-crafted final speech included a point-by-point refutation of the charges against him and a stream of witticisms, which, if genuine, must have been prepared and rehearsed with an eye to posterity.

There are several accounts of Raleigh's death. The one reproduced here was taken down by Mr Henley, one of the clerks of Sir Julius Caesar, the Master of the Rolls. As well as ruling contentiously against John Milward's marriage in the High Court of Delegates (see document 12) and being a commissioner in the case of the Essex divorce (see document 13), Caesar was one of the commissioners appointed to hear Raleigh's case and to condemn him; he was also prominent in the group of governors attempting to order James' finances. It is hard to imagine there was no link between these two offices. Raleigh's greatest error was not offending Spain, writing against the tyranny of Princes, providing a focus and figurehead for malcontents of all complexions, or even popularizing tobacco, but failing to return from his voyage laden with the gold of the Orinoco.

THE ACCOUNT CONCLUDES:

...I will make bold (my honourable lords) to take my leave, having a long journey to undergo and an assured hope to be quickly there.

Then he called for the Executioner who, kneeling down, he laid both his hands upon his shoulders, heartily forgiving him and demanding his Axe, he [the executioner] looked wildly and fearfully about him, why, quoth [said] Sir Walter, do you think I am afraid of it, who being commanded so to do gave it into his hands, then Sir Walter taking and trying with his thumb the sharpness of the edge, Here is, quoth he, a Physician that can cure all diseases, and

Second page
so re-delivering it again, prepared himself for the Block, and there being a dispute by some that his face should lie towards the East, he answered, so the heart be right it is no matter where the head lies. Then the headsman asking whether he should not cut his waistcoat, because it came too high up into his neck, to which Sir Walter answered, must thou [you must] cut my flesh, and do you fear to cut my waistcoat. Then laying his head on the block after his general Adieu at the first stroke he was quite dead, yet there were two blows given.

The verses read:

Made by Sir W Raleigh the morning before his death
and delivered to the Dean of Westminster a little before his end.

Even such is time, which takes in trust
Our youth, our joys and all we have
And pays us but with age and dust
Who in the dark and silent grave
When we have wandered all our ways
Shuts up the story of our days
And from which earth and grave and dust
The Lord shall raise me up I trust

... to some, and casting ...
therefore humbly, and hartely request mee, desiring the great God
of Heaven to forgive mee, to have mercy upon mee, in Christes Christ
whose blood is the Gate of Heaven, and by whose death and Meritts
that Gate is opened to all that trust in him.

I mee now bidd you all farewell Desiring you to pray ...
you to pray for mee, and I will goe make my ... on my
God, and prepare my selfe for the world to come.

I will make bold (my honourable Lord) to take my leave, having a
long iourney, &, to undergoe, and an assured hope to bee quietly ...

Then he called to the Executioner, who kneeling downe laid both
his hands upon his shoulders hartily, forgiving him, & demanding
his Axe, who looking wishly and carefully about him. Why Guy
(Sir Walter) thinkest thou I am afraid of it, who being demanded
so to doe, hee gave it pp into his handes. Then Sir Walter
taking and proving to his hand the Sharpnes of the Edge
sayd it (quoth hee) a Phisition that cures all diseases, and ...

for redelivering it Againe prepared himselfe to the Blocke
And there being a Dispute by some that his face should lye
towards the East, hee answeared, so the heart bee right, it is no
matter whi the head is.

This headsman asking whether hee should Putt his Cloke
because his hands ..., vp into the wist: To my Sir Walter
Answeared, ... thou Putt my Ax, &c, and dost thou feare
to Putt my Masterie.

Then laying his heade on the Blocke (after his generall
Adiew) at the first stroke hee was quite Dead, and yet
... were two blowes given.

Made by Sr Wr Raleigh the
morning before his death and ...
delivered to the deane of
West minster a little before his death

Oct: 29, 1618

Even such is time, which takes in trust
our youth, our joyes and all we have
And payes us but with age and dust
who in the darke and silent grave
when we have wandred all our wayes
shutts up the storye of our dayes
And from which earth and grave and dust
The Lord shall rayse me up I trust

Portrait of George Villiers, 1st Duke of Buckingham, by Daniel Mytens. Portraits of Villiers generally make a great deal of his legs, and he capered his way to prominence, obliging when James, bored with the masque as usual, had demanded dancing. Their letters leave little room for doubt that he and the King were lovers, at least before Villiers' marriage, and that the King's love endured longer than his favourite's. This led to stories that Villiers had tired of James and even poisoned him. This seems unlikely since the King was dying anyway and Villiers' grief at his death seems to have been genuine, but the allegation was repeated by Buckingham's enemies long afterwards.

Charles himself became fiercely anti-Spanish and determined to govern the failing King and persuade him into a war with Spain.

James eventually consulted Parliament on the issue of the Spanish marriage in February 1624, which might seem ironic since he had forbidden it to interfere in foreign policy in 1621. In fact, he was being consistent as it was usually his impulse, when receiving advice he did not like, even if it came from his favourite and his son, to seek more advice from another source. Parliament was naturally anti-Spanish, but less inclined than the Prince and Villiers to rush into war. Read James' secret letter to Edward Conway: document 20, *'Pardon me...'*. After spending his reign exalting the dignity of royalty and the prestige of his favourites, and preserving peace against great odds, James ended it writing in fear of Charles and Villiers, broken by financial necessity and on the verge of war with the power he had tried most strenuously to cultivate.

ILLNESS, DEATH AND LEGACY

In the warm dry summer of 1624 James was largely free of the arthritis which had plagued him for many years, but it returned in the autumn. The treaty that bound Prince Charles to Henrietta Maria of France in September was stamped because James could not sign it. The reality of the French match was as unpopular as the prospect of the Spanish one had been.

James was briefly at Whitehall for Christmas 1624, then out again to his favourite hunting spots at Royston and Newmarket. In his final decline his symptoms multiplied. There is evidence that he suffered a stroke and dysentery. Official accounts of his godly end masked a death which must have been physically horrible.

He died on 27 March 1625 and the final great royal pageant, his funeral procession, was held in lavish splendour on 7 May. Maintaining the link with Henry VII he had made at the time of the proposed union of England and Scotland, James had appropriated Henry's chapel in Westminster Abbey. In a suitable clash of symbolism and reality his body was later found lodged awkwardly between Henry and Elizabeth of York. Whereas the death of Queen Elizabeth in 1603 had provoked little genuine mourning in an England that had grown tired of her, in Charles I's reign, the anniversary of Elizabeth's coronation day would be celebrated when the reigning monarch's was not. Elizabeth's reputation remained intact partly because her childlessness and reluctance to name her successor freed her from responsibility for what happened next. James' dynasty, which seemed his greatest asset in 1603, has not helped his reputation.

Rubens ceiling, central panel: *Apotheosis of James I*, Banqueting House, Whitehall. The old Banqueting House had burned down in 1619 when masque costumes caught fire. The new building was designed by Inigo Jones and completed in 1622. The magnificent ceiling paintings by Sir Peter Paul Rubens, for which the building is renowned, were commissioned by 'Baby Charles' to celebrate his father's life and wise government, and installed by 1636. The Banqueting House later became the scene of Charles' execution. In the Apotheosis itself (right) James is shown being raised to the heavens by Justice, on his left, while his symbols of earthly majesty, the crown and orb, are borne away by cherubs.

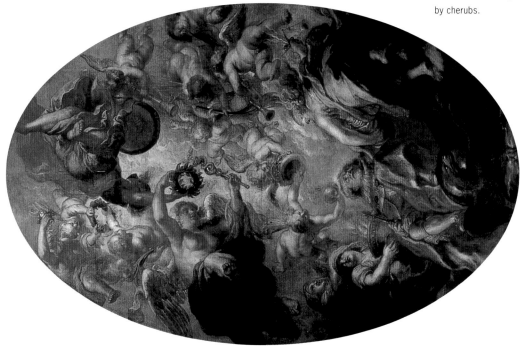

A letter from James to Edward Conway, 4 April 1624. This two-page letter, in James' failing hand, betrays something of the weakness of his position at the end of his reign. Here he is being pressured by his son, Prince Charles and his favourite, George Villiers, Duke of Buckingham into a war with Spain, a war he had gone to such great lengths throughout his reign to avoid.

James' son and his favourite appeared to have the backing of Parliament, though Parliament was more enthusiastic about calling for war against Spain than funding it. Brow-beaten by his closest advisers and mistrustful of Parliament, James tries to evade the former and gauge the mood of the latter through Conway, a Secretary of State appointed through Villiers' influence, who James complained 'could not write'. One of James' strengths had been dealing with political opponents face to face; he had done it in Scotland, again at the Hampton Court conference, and he had wanted to face the Gunpowder Plotters. Now he was reduced to relying on hearsay and third parties he did not care for. Charles and Villiers began to amend James' speeches to 'clarify' them in his absence. Villiers especially had become too powerful for the King to stop. The letter shows signs of James' physical frailty but little sign of mental deterioration or lack of judgement, though he is in a weak position. There is still the familiar train of logical reasoning, trepidation mixed with good sense and naivety with practised knowledge of the motivations and likely actions of those around him.

The packet referred to in the letter was that ending the treaties with Spain, whose messenger had already been detained in James' agony of uncertainty on this point. Parliament's petition, also mentioned here, urged that no marriage treaty should bring religious toleration for English Catholics.

JAMES WROTE:

Pardon me the breaking of this hour, for it is a fault I seldom commit; but my son's being here and a number of people that came with him so plied me with business as I had never leisure till now to write to you. My son will inform you as he finds the lower house inclined in this business, that you may advertise [notify] me accordingly, I mean whether they will go on with the subsidies according to their promise, and trust to my wisdom and discretion in answering their petition; or if they will make it in effect a condition *sine qua non*, though not say it plainly. I hope you will likewise do all you can to discover this, for if I may be sure that they mean to keep their promise to me, let the packet go on. Otherwise it were [there is] no reason I should be bound and they leap free and leave me naked and without help.

Though I have commanded my son to acquaint you with what he can discover,

The letter continues:

yet he knows not of these my private directions to you. All this I must commit to your secrecy, discretion, and diligence. The short and the long is that if I may be sure that their passing of the subsidies will not depend upon my answer to their petition, let the post go, post haste post [let the messenger go as quickly as possible]. But if they will not move without first having their will in that, no reason they should break their promise and I still be bound. Farewell. James R.

pardon me the breaking of this howre, for it is a faulte

47

I seeldome comitte, but my sonnis being heere & a nombre

of people that came with him so plued me with bussienesse

as I hadde neuer laaser till now, to wryte vnto

you, my sonne will informe you as he fyndes the

lower howse enclyned in this bussienesse, that ye

maye aduertishe me accordinglie, I meane, quhither

according to thaire promeise

thaye will goe on with the subsideis & truste to my

wisedome & discretion in answring thaire pe=

in effect

tition, or if thaye will make it a condition sine qua

thogh it

non, & noe saye plainlie, I hoape ye will lyke it, ye aye

for

doe all ye can to discouer this, if I maye be sure that

thaye meane to keepe thaire promeise to me, lette the

paquette goe on, other wayes it waire no reason

I showlde be bownde & thaye leape free & leaue,

nowe

me naked & without helpe, thogh I haue comandit

my sonne to aquainte you with quhat he can discouer

Who's Who

Lancelot Andrewes (1555–1626). Bishop of Chichester (1605), Ely (1609) and Winchester (1619); prominent at the Hampton Court conference he became general editor of the Authorized Version of the Bible. One of the commissioners appointed to consider the Essex divorce, he is said to have opposed it until pressured by the King. His mixture of learning and sophistication appealed greatly to James who believed his sermons to be divinely inspired. James is said to have called for him in his last illness, but Andrewes was himself too ill to attend.

Robert Armyn (c.1570–1615). Writer and comic actor. Mentioned in the royal patent to The King's Men in 1603. Thought to have played the roles of Feste in *Twelfth Night*, Autolycus in *The Winter's Tale* and the Fool in *King Lear*.

Anthony Babington (1561–86). Former page to Mary Queen of Scots, he became involved in the conspiracy which bears his name in 1585 and was executed in the following year. Mary's implication in the plot led to her own execution.

Francis Bacon (1561–1626). One of many to receive a knighthood in 1603. Solicitor-General (1607), Attorney-General (1613), Lord Keeper (1617), Lord Chancellor and Baron Verulam, (1618), Viscount St Albans (1621). In 1621 he was found guilty of 23 counts of corruption, fined, and banned from public office. Also a writer and philosopher, he tried and failed to interest James and his court in inductive philosophy.

Richard Bancroft (1544–1610). Bishop of London (1597) and Archbishop of Canterbury (1604), he was the principal spokesman of the bishops at the Hampton Court conference. Archbishop of Canterbury (1604). He also opposed the new translation of the Bible but became its 'overseer'.

Richard Burbage (c.1571–1619). Actor, prominent in the Lord Chamberlain's Company then The King's Men. One of those who tore down the Theatre and carried it across the river to be rebuilt as the Globe. Played Richard III, Hamlet, Othello and King Lear.

Julius Caesar (1558–1636). Judge and Master of the Rolls. Served James in a number of judicial and administrative capacities; a commissioner appointed to examine (and approve) the Essex divorce and examine (and condemn) Sir Walter Raleigh. One of the knights created in 1603, he was appointed Chancellor of the Exchequer in 1606 and Master of the Rolls in 1614. His judgement in the High Court of Delegates against John Milward occasioned the Star Chamber investigation into whether his judgement had been swayed by perjured evidence and Chapman's play.

Robert Carr, Viscount Rochester, Earl of Somerset (1585?–1645). Rapidly elevated by James after his adoption as favourite. Knighted in December 1607 and given the estate of Sherborne, Dorset formerly owned by Sir Walter Raleigh. Created Viscount Rochester and Lord High Treasurer of Scotland in 1611, and a Privy Councillor in 1612. After the Essex divorce, he was made Earl of Somerset so that he could marry Frances Howard and she could remain a Countess. Pleaded not guilty to the murder of Sir Thomas Overbury, found guilty, condemned to death, but reprieved. Imprisoned with his wife until 1622.

Robert Catesby (1573–1605). A sound inheritance and a rich marriage had made him a wealthy man but he was one of those Catholics imprisoned and heavily fined for his part in the Essex rebellion in 1601. A forceful and magnetic personality who powered the Gunpowder Plot and drew others into it. Killed by the same shot that killed Thomas Percy at Holbeach.

Robert Cecil, Earl of Salisbury (1563–1612). Second son of William Cecil, Lord Burghley. Trained by his father for the royal service, he became Principal Secretary in 1596 and Lord Keeper of the Privy Seal by 1601. Subsequently Earl of Salisbury (1605) and Lord Treasurer (1608). James swapped Hatfield House for Cecil's much greater estate at Theobalds. Supreme in James' government, he was blamed by the King for the failure of the Great Contract (1610) and was the subject of crowing denigration after his death.

John Chamberlain (1554–1628). Newsgatherer, court intelligencer and letter-writer. Well educated and well connected, he lodged with friends or relatives close to St Paul's Cathedral, London's prime location for the exchange of news. He watched and listened for 30 years sending news to his friends, most frequently and famously to Sir Dudley Carleton, a diplomat.

George Chapman (1559–1634?). Poet and playwright. His lost play *The Old Joiner of Aldgate* dramatized the events in the Milward case and he twice gave evidence in Star Chamber. Often had the misfortune to acquire literary patrons just before they died or fell from favour. He continued to dedicate work to Carr after his fall from favour. Imprisoned with John Marston and Ben Jonson for scurrilous remarks about the Scots in their comedy *Eastward Ho!*.

Robert Cotton (1571–1631). Antiquarian and manuscript collector, helped found the Society of Antiquaries around 1586. Knighted at James' coronation and created Baronet in 1611. A Member of Parliament, firstly under the patronage of the Howard family, then of Carr. In 1616 he was imprisoned in the Tower of London for five months because of advice he had given to Carr during the Overbury investigation; thereafter increasingly identified with those opposed to James' government and the power of Villiers. Greeted Charles I on his accession not with another pedigree but with a study of the reign of Henry III widely interpreted as a

plea to Charles to reform his government. Cotton's library came to be seen as politically dangerous and was periodically closed. Cotton's grandson presented his collections to the nation in 1700, and, though they suffered fire in 1730, they now form an important part of the British Library.

Robert Devereux, 2nd Earl of Essex (1566–1601). Successor to his stepfather, Robert Dudley, Earl of Leicester as Queen Elizabeth's chief favourite. Courted by James because of his influence with the Queen, he was disgraced after ignoring Elizabeth's orders while campaigning in Ireland. Essex became the popular figurehead of a diverse group of malcontents. Determined to unseat Robert Cecil, who he blamed for his failures, he led an abortive rising against Elizabeth's government in London in February 1601 and was executed.

Robert Devereux, 3rd Earl of Essex (1591–1646). Soldier, restored to his titles by James after having lost them through his father, the 2nd Earl's disgrace. Encouraged by James in his marriage to Frances Howard in 1606, he served overseas from 1607 to 1609, when his wife began her affair with Robert Carr. After the dissolution of their marriage he fought for Frederick, Elector Palatine in the Rhineland and took part in the bungled raid on Cadiz in 1625. He emerged as a prominent critic of Charles' government on his return and accepted the post of General in the Parliamentarian army on the outbreak of Civil War.

Guy Fawkes (1570–1606). Gunpowder Plotter. Born in York of Protestant parents but accepted the Catholic faith of a stepfather. Crossed to Flanders in 1593 and joined the Spanish forces there. Returned to England in 1604 and in May was enlisted in Catesby's conspiracy.

Lawrence Fletcher (d.1608). James' favourite actor; part of a touring company which James supported when the Kirk threatened to suppress the players in November 1599. Mentioned both on the patent to The King's Men and in the account for cloth given to them for the coronation procession; evidence that he actually acted with the company is harder to come by.

Simon Forman (1552–1611). Astrologer and doctor. Abandoned his apprenticeship as a grocer to practise 'physic and magic'. Settled in London in 1589 where he made his reputation, treating plague victims, including himself and his family, when many doctors fled the city. His success brought him into conflict with the College of Physicians and he suffered several periods of imprisonment, until he was licensed as a doctor by Cambridge University in 1603. Wild rumours spread about him after his death, not least about his role in the Overbury poisoning. Forman kept a diary of his practice and a *Book of Plays* containing records of performances at the Globe in 1611.

Samuel Harsnet (1561–1631). Archbishop of York from 1628. Served as chaplain to Bishop Bancroft. In this capacity he licensed books for the press, including Hayward's history of the reign of Henry IV, which appeared to justify rebellion. He was able to convince the Council that he had not perceived the political implications of the narrative. In 1603 he published *A Declaration of Egregious Popish Impostures*, which exposed the methods of priests provoking simulated demonic possession and then winning converts by 'curing' it through exorcism. Some of the vocabulary of this work appears in the feigned lunacy of Edgar in *King Lear*. Later Bishop of Chichester (1609) and Norwich (1619) before his elevation to York.

Francis Stewart Hepburn, 5th Earl of Bothwell (d.1624). Nephew of the 4th Earl of Bothwell. Wild and dangerous opponent of James in Scotland; he was anxious that Mary Queen of Scots' death should be avenged by an invasion of England. Imprisoned for witchcraft after the trials at North Berwick, he escaped from captivity in 1591, and was deprived by Parliament of his lands and titles. As an outlaw he was spectacular:

in 1591 he attempted to seize Holyrood palace, and in 1593 he captured the King, forcing from him a promise of pardon. Although James failed to apprehend him, he was forced to take refuge abroad. He died at Naples in poverty.

James Hepburn, 4th Earl of Bothwell (c.1535–78). A Privy Councillor on Mary Queen of Scots' return to Scotland, he became one of her closest advisers. He married, but then divorced in doubtful circumstances, when the prospect arose of marrying the Queen. Instrumental in the murder of Darnley, he was rewarded with the Dukedom of Orkney. Darnley's father, the Earl of Lennox led an attempt to prosecute Bothwell for the murder, but found a trial engineered by the Queen to acquit him. Bothwell's secret marriage to Mary was declared to be invalid when Mary's later betrothal to the Duke of Norfolk was mooted. After Mary's defeat and imprisonment, Bothwell contemplated a life of piracy in Shetland, finally fleeing to Denmark, where he was imprisoned. His fortunes waned with Mary's; his confinement becoming gradually closer and less congenial until his death.

Frances Howard, Countess of Essex, Countess of Somerset (1592–1632). Married the third Earl of Essex when she was 13 and he 14. Encouraged in her affair with Robert Carr by her family. Essex tried to remove her from the court to the country in 1610, prompting her action for annulment of the marriage. Married Carr in December 1613, but investigations into the death of Sir Thomas Overbury led to her trial for murder with her husband in 1616. Unlike her husband she pleaded guilty.

Hugh O'Neill, Earl of Tyrone (1540?–1616). Appointed by Queen Elizabeth as defender of English interests in Ulster, he later became a leading rebel against English rule. Successful in battle over nearly a decade he finally submitted in 1603, shortly before Elizabeth's death. As King of Scotland, James cultivated Tyrone while seeming publicly to disapprove of his actions. James welcomed him to the English court in 1603, but Tyrone continued to talk rebellion, and, fearing a sudden summons from James in 1607 meant imprisonment, fled to France and then Rome.

Thomas Overbury (1581–1613). Writer and murder victim. Met Robert Carr in Edinburgh in 1601. With Carr's sudden rise to favour Overbury renewed the friendship in 1607, acting as Carr's secretary. A member of the anti-Spanish party, Overbury initially tried to steer his friend away from involvement with the Howard family, but was drawn into the affair with Frances Howard, even helping to compose his master's love letters. Carr was Overbury's only protection against the many enemies his pride and vanity had made him, and when they fell out over the Essex divorce and Carr's proposed marriage, he became very vulnerable. Assaulted in mind and body, by lying letters and poisoned food while imprisoned in the Tower of London, he finally succumbed to a poisoned enema. An enquiry into his death eventually convicted those of his principal opponents who were still alive. His publications, including *A Wife*, a treatise on the ideal marriage, proved very popular after his death.

William Parker, Lord Monteagle (1576–1622). Catholic with property in Warwickshire, Worcestershire and Essex. Fought in Ireland under the Earl of Essex and supported the Essex rebellion; he was imprisoned in the Tower of London for eight months and fined £8,000. On his release Catesby contacted him. In the winter of 1604–5 he told the King he was prepared to abjure his Catholicism, and he became eligible to sit in the House of Lords. For his action in exposing the Gunpowder Plot he was given landed property and an annual pension of £500. He invested substantially in the Virginia Company, joining its council in 1609.

Henry Percy, 9th Earl of Northumberland (1564–1631). Head of one of England's great Catholic families though he professed not to be a Catholic himself. Born at Tynemouth but not allowed to live in or visit the north of England after the execution of his uncle, the seventh Earl, following the Northern Rebellion in 1572. Succeeded to the title in 1585 when his father, the eighth Earl allegedly shot himself through the heart while imprisoned in the Tower of London on suspicion of complicity in the plots surrounding Mary Queen of Scots. Fought in the Netherlands and against the Armada. Famous in peacetime for his love of scientific experiment, he earned the popular title 'The Wizard Earl'. Restored to political prominence after his role in ensuring James' peaceful succession, the Earl was compromised by strong circumstantial evidence linking him to Thomas Percy at the time of the Gunpowder Plot. He was sent to the Tower, but lived there in some style with his servants and his books. Released under an amnesty after 16 years in prison, he died on 5 November 1631, still insisting he had never shared the religious faith of the plotters.

Thomas Percy (c.1560–1605). Gunpowder Plotter. A distant cousin of the Earl of Northumberland, Percy served his kinsman as chief agent for his estates in the north, and was constable of Alnwick Castle from 1596. Most of the facts of Percy's life are disputed; the extent to which he embezzled from his master to finance a Catholic uprising and, especially, how much contact he had with Robert Cecil before the plot came to light. His connection with the Earl was one of the government's chief leads in investigating the power behind the plot, but Percy's death at Holbeach made proving a formal link much more difficult.

Pocahontas (c.1595–1617). Matoaka, daughter of Powhatan, chief of the confederacy of Algonquin tribes in Virginia. Nicknamed and generally known as Pocahontas, a reference to her playfulness as a child. Reputed to have rescued Captain John Smith from sacrificial death in her father's camp, she became a friend of Smith and a protector of the colonists. Leaving her father's lands she was discovered and taken hostage by a trading expedition from Jamestown, which thought she might be used to ensure Powhatan's good behaviour. She was not ransomed but remained with the colonists. She was converted to Christianity, baptized 'Rebecca' and married John Rolfe. After her marriage she helped establish a peace between the Virginians and the settlers, which lasted until 1622.

Walter Raleigh (1552–1618). Said to have advocated a Commonwealth after the death of Elizabeth I rather than have a Scottish king of England, prompting James to pun 'O my soule, mon, I have heard rawly of thee'. He never recovered the King's esteem. Feigned leprosy to delay his journey from his West Country estates to imprisonment in London, an imposture detected at Salisbury by Richard Haydock the 'sleeping preacher', who took his pulse. After his execution his widow kept his embalmed head.

John Rolfe (c.1585–1622). Colonist, tobacco-planter and husband of Pocahontas. Sailed for Jamestown in 1609 and was wrecked in Bermuda on the way. A daughter 'Bermuda' was born and died there. His wife was dead by 1613. Finally arriving at Jamestown, he began planting West Indian tobacco, which proved a great success and broke the Spanish monopoly on the Caribbean variety. After his marriage to Pocahontas, Rolfe became Secretary of the colony and wrote *A True Relation of the State of Virginia*, as well as a letter to James about the prospects for the tobacco industry. He was not invited to court when Pocahontas went to the masque. After Pocahontas died Rolfe remarried and grew in prominence in the colony.

Henry Stuart, Lord Darnley, Earl of Ross, Duke of Albany (1545–67). James' father. Darnley was entertained at the French court as a possible heir to the kingdoms of England and Scotland in his own right: his father was the Earl of Lennox and his mother was the daughter of Margaret Tudor by her second marriage to the Earl of Angus. Darnley married Mary Queen of Scots in 1565. He proved a poor councillor to his wife but was passionately jealous of those she took into her confidence when he failed her. The birth of James helped to reconcile the couple temporarily, but Darnley made powerful enemies. When the house he was lodged in, Kirk o' Fields in Edinburgh, was destroyed in an enormous gunpowder explosion in February 1567, his body was discovered in the garden of the house, free of any marks associated with an explosion, but apparently strangled.

George Villiers, Duke of Buckingham (1592–1628). Courtier and politician. Within a month of first meeting the King in August 1614 he was being recognized as the new court favourite. He was knighted in April 1615, made Viscount Villiers in 1616, Earl of Buckingham in 1617 and Marquis in 1618. He began to sell honours as well as to receive them. The King encouraged his friendship with Prince Charles, and Villiers arranged their secret journey to Spain to further Charles' marriage plans. Despite James' misgivings about the escapade, he made Villiers Duke of Buckingham when the pair returned safely. Their letters leave little room for doubt that Villiers and the King had a physical relationship and that the favourite began to rule the King. He continued to enjoy great influence with Charles after James' death. Resented at court for the suddenness of his rise and the extent of his power, and hated in the country for a series of bungled foreign policy forays, he was assassinated in 1628.

The Houses of Tudor and Stuart

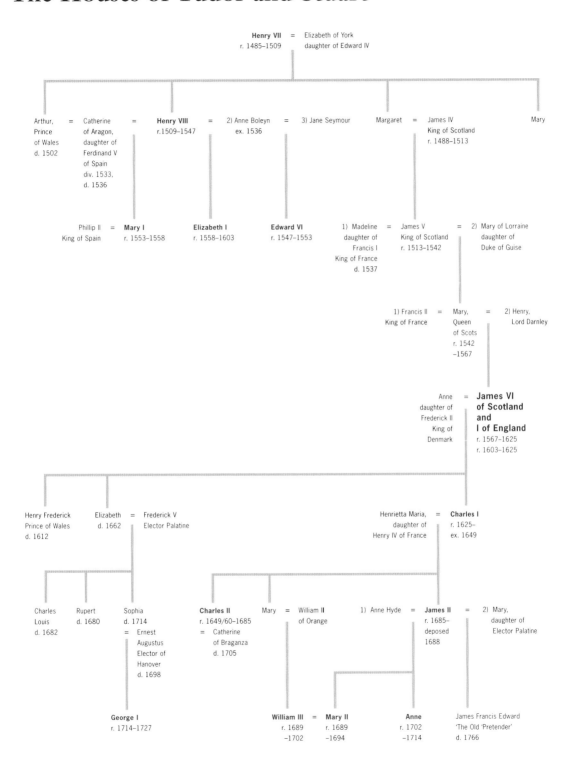

Chronology

1566	**19 June** Birth of James at Edinburgh Castle.
	17 December Baptism of James at Stirling Castle.
1567	**10 February** Murder of James' father, Lord Darnley, at Kirk o' Fields, near Edinburgh.
	15 May Mary Queen of Scots marries James Hepburn, 4th Earl of Bothwell.
	15 June Mary Queen of Scots defeated by Protestant Lords at the Battle of Carberry Hill.
	24 July Abdication of Mary Queen of Scots.
	29 July Coronation of James as King of Scots. In the care and custody of John Erskine, 1st /6th Earl of Mar.
	22 August James Stewart, Earl of Moray, half-brother of Mary Queen of Scots, proclaimed Regent of Scotland.
1568	Flight of Mary Queen of Scots to England.
1570	**22 January** Murder of Regent Moray.
	12 July Matthew Stuart, Earl of Lennox appointed Regent with the backing of Elizabeth I.
1571	**3 September** Regent Lennox murdered by supporters of Mary. Earl of Mar appointed Regent, dies a year later. Real power passes to James Douglas, Earl of Morton.
1578	James begins to rule in his own right. Morton forced from power.
1579	Arrival at court and rise of James' first favourite, Esmé Stuart, created Duke of Lennox.
1581	**2 June** Execution of Regent Morton for his part in the death of Lord Darnley.

1582	**22 August** James abducted by the 2nd/7th Earl of Mar and the Earl of Gowrie and taken to Ruthven Castle. Exile of Lennox.
1583	**27 June** James escapes from Ruthven. Rise of James Stewart, Earl of Arran, as James' favourite and chief councillor.
1585	Fall of the Earl of Arran.
1587	**9 February** Execution of Mary Queen of Scots.
1589	**20 August** James marries Anne of Denmark by proxy in Copenhagen.
	23 November Marriage celebrated in person in Oslo.
1590	Anne, a Lutheran in Denmark, becomes a Catholic in Scotland.
1590–1	North Berwick witch trials. Outlawry of Francis, 5th Earl of Bothwell.
1594	**19 February** Birth of Prince Henry.
1596	**19 August** Birth of Princess Elizabeth. The 'Octavians' appointed.
1598	James writes *Basilikon Doron* (a secret edition of seven copies is produced in 1599).
1600	**5 August** The Gowrie Conspiracy.
	19 November Birth of Prince Charles.
1601	**9 February** Essex rebellion takes place.
1603	**March** Surrender of the Earl of Tyrone.
	24 March Death of Queen Elizabeth. James proclaimed king in London.
	April Millenary Petition presented to James.
	25 July James crowned in Westminster Abbey.

1604   **14 January** Hampton Court conference begins.

            15 March Royal progress through London.

            March–July Parliamentary session. Union of England and Scotland proposed.

            August Treaty of London ends war with Spain.

1605   **26 October** Monteagle receives his letter warning of the Gunpowder Plot.

            5 November Discovery of the Gunpowder Plot.

1606–7   Parliament debates union of England and Scotland.

1607   **September** Flight of the Earls of Tyrone and Tyrconnel from Ireland.

1608   Robert Cecil appointed Lord Treasurer, sets out new and revived Crown money-raising measures.

            Appointment of Commissioners for Ulster.

1610   **May** Assassination of Henry IV of France.

            October Failure of The Great Contract.

1611   Publication of the King James Bible.

1612   **12 May** Death of Robert Cecil.

            6 November Death of Prince Henry.

1613   **14 February** Marriage of Princess Elizabeth to Frederick, Elector Palatine.

            15 September Death of Sir Thomas Overbury in the Tower.

            25 September The Essex divorce granted.

            26 December Somerset marriage takes place.

1614	**April–June** Impasse between James and the Parliament, which passed no Bills, known as the 'Addled Parliament'. James rules without Parliament until 1621.
1615–16	Trials take place of those involved in Sir Thomas Overbury's murder.
1616	**March** Release of Sir Walter Raleigh for Guiana expedition.
	July Trial and conviction of the Earl and Countess of Somerset, in the Overbury case.
1616–17	Pocahontas at court.
1617	**1 January** George Villiers created Earl of Buckingham.
	Scottish progress.
1618	**1 January** George Villiers created Marquis of Buckingham.
	July Invasion of Bohemia by Imperial army against Protestant government in Prague. Thirty Years' War begins.
	29 October Execution of Sir Walter Raleigh.
1619	**2 March** Death of Anne of Denmark.
	Banqueting House burns down.
	September Frederick, Elector Palatine, accepts the Crown of Bohemia.
1620	**August** Palatinate invaded by Imperial troops.
	October King Frederick of Bohemia expelled from his kingdom after the Battle of the White Mountain.
	December Pilgrim Fathers establish a colony at Plymouth, New England.

1621	**January–June** James' third Parliament, first session. Debates on monopolies, impeachment of Bacon.
	June Arrest of Sir Edwin Sandys and the Earls of Oxford and Southampton for opposition in Parliament.
1622	**March** Massacre of Jamestown settlers; end of 'The Peace of Pocahontas'.
1623	**March–October** Mission of Charles and Villiers to Spain.
	May Villiers created Duke of Buckingham.
1624	**February–May** James' fourth and last Parliament. Pressure for war against Spain. Monopolies Act.
1624	**June** Collapse of the Virginia Company.
	November Treaty with France.
1625	**27 March** Death of James at Theobalds, Hertfordshire.
	7 May James' funeral, estimated to cost £50,000.

Further Reading

G. P. V. Aikrigg, *Letters of King James VI and I* (University of California Press, 1984). Transcribes many of James' letters from a variety of sources with helpful introductory paragraphs giving context of letters.

A. Bellany, *The Politics of Court Scandal in Early Modern England* (Cambridge University Press, 2002). Scholarly study of the Overbury scandal and 'news culture'.

C. Bingham, *James I of England* (Weidenfeld & Nicolson, 1981). Enjoyable biography, a little coy about its sources. There is a companion volume about James' reign before 1603, published in 1979.

J. Cook, *Dr Simon Forman: a most notorious physician* (Chatto and Windus, 2001). Based on Forman's diaries, a useful and engaging account of the man himself and the London of the first part of James' reign in England.

J. Cramsie, *Kingship and Crown Finance Under James VI and I* (Boydell Press, 2002). Scholarly but refreshing analysis of one of the great issues of the reign.

J. F. Larkin and P. L. Hughes (eds), *Stuart Royal Proclamations* (Clarendon Press, 1973). Transcribes and annotates proclamations with helpful introductory paragraphs giving context.

R. Lockyer, *James VI and I* (Longman, 1998). Accessible, scholarly and a useful corrective to the traditional critical view of James.

D. Matthew, *James I* (Eyre and Spottiswoode, 1967). Flowery but fun. Good on James' literary productions.

N. E. McClure, *The Letters of John Chamberlain* (Philadelphia, The American Philosophical Society, 1939). Transcribes and usefully annotates a vital source of inside information and gossip for the period. Many of the original letters are preserved among the State Papers in the National Archives.

M. Nicholls, *Investigating the Gunpowder Plot* (Manchester University Press, 1991). A sensible well-sourced book in a sea of silly, badly sourced books. Especially strong on the Percy connection.

J. A. Sharpe, *The Bewitching of Anne Gunter* (Profile Books, 1999). Faithful to its sources, social history and true crime mystery combined.

C. J. Sisson, *The Lost Plays of Shakespeare's Age* (Humanities Press, 1936). Reconstructs lost plays from documentary sources, including Chapman's *The Old Joiner of Aldgate*.

A. Stewart, *The Cradle King: A Life of James VI and I* (Chatto and Windus, 2003). A good modern biography especially strong on James' early life.

D. H. Wilson, *James VI and I* (Jonathan Cape, 1956). Still the best single-volume biography, meticulous and readable, but marred by the author's vehement dislike of his subject.

J. Wormald, *Court, Kirk and Community: Scotland 1470–1625* (New History of Scotland, Edinburgh University Press, 1991). Excellent book on the Scottish background by one of the leading historians of James' reign.

Picture Credits

Illustrations

Cover: by courtesy of the National Portrait Gallery, London; pp. i and x Galleria degli Uffizi, Florence, Italy/Bridgeman Art Library;
pp. ii and 72–3 by permission of the British Library (MS. Add. 36932); p. 2 Private Collection/Gavin Graham Gallery, London, UK/Bridgeman Art Library; p. 5 Collections/Dennis Barnes;
p. 6 by permission of the British Museum, London; p. 11 by permission of the British Library (BL C 107 dg 25); p. 15 by courtesy of the National Portrait Gallery, London; p. 22 National Museums of Scotland/Bridgeman Art Library;
p. 24 Collections/Philip Craven; p. 25 by permission of the British Library (BL C 35.113);
p. 28 Private Collection/Bridgeman Art Library;
p. 29 by permission of the British Library (BL WP 7332); p. 32 by permission of the British Library (BL WP 7332); p. 34 by permission of the British Library (BL C.37 f. 36);
p. 40 Collections/Brian Shuel; p. 44 Private Collection/Bridgeman Art Library;
p. 45 by permission of the British Library (BL 11266); p. 48 Private Collection/Bridgeman Art Library; p. 49 by permission of the British Library (BL 11266);
p. 53 Private Collection/Bridgeman Art Library;
p. 58 Society of Antiquaries, London/Bridgeman Art Library; p. 59 by permission of the British Library (BL 292); p. 62 by permission of the British Library (BL 292 f. 37);
p. 65 Collections/Oliver Benn; p. 68 Wallace Collection, London, UK/Bridgeman Art Library;
p. 70 Chateau de Beauregard, France/Peter Willi/Bridgeman Art Library; p. 71 by permission of the Guildhall Library, Corporation of London;
p. 74 Private Collection/Bridgeman Art Library;
p. 75 The Roxburghe Ballads; p. 82 by permission of the British Library (BL 236);
p. 81 Kunsthistorisches Museum, Vienna, Austria/Bridgeman Art Library; p. 86 Devonshire Collection, Chatsworth. Reproduced by permission of the Duke of Devonshire and the Chatsworth Settlement Trustees;

p. 96 Collections/James Bartholomew;
p. 97 © Society of Antiquaries, London;
p. 100 Private Collection/Christie's Images/Bridgeman Art Library; p. 101 Crown copyright: Historic Royal Palaces

All other images are from The National Archives:
Cover and pp. v and 56 KB 27/1522/2;
p. iii SC13/N4; p. iv MPF 1/366;
p. 14 SC 13/T245; p. 18 PRO 30/25/205;
p. 19 AO 3/908/13; p. 33 WO 78/418;
p. 43 SP 14/216; p. 54 SP 14/216;
p. 63 MPH 1/213; p. 78 MPG 1/284;
p. 88 E 30/1705; p. 92 MPF 1/51

Picture research by Deborah Pownall.

Original documents

All documents are held in The National Archives.

Index